THE
SHADOW
WORK
WORKBOOK AND JOURNAL

How To Meet Your True Self

Integrate & Transcend Your Dark Side Through Self-Discovery Exercises

Deep Journal Prompts for Inner Child Soothing, Healing & Growth

Samantha Jones

BOOK SQUARE PUBLISHING

First Printing Edition, 2023
Printed in the United States of America
Available from Amazon.com and other retail outlet

What people have been saying...

"I appreciate the detailed explanations of each archetype before you go into thought provoking or exploration questions leading to the journal prompt. There are a few people that come for counseling seeking a deeper understanding of oneself and I think this is a great way of having them explore different aspects of their personality. But really anyone and everyone can use it for personal growth. Great book!"

Samar, Licensed Professional Counselor Associate

"I absolutely loved this shadow work book/guide! I think it's beautifully put together, and I love how it explains what shadow work is first, and then flows into the different types of shadows, and then into the work itself. It's incredibly detailed and also easy to follow. Anyone looking for this type of work will definitely receive so much from this! It's such an important piece of our journey and not one that is easily stepped into. Many people are afraid to look at these places, so this guide will be a beautiful companion for their journey!!"

Jennifer, Transformative Coach

"This workbook absolutely enhances The work I undertake with clients that are interested in Self Awareness, development and getting to flow with their authentic aspect of self. Trying to explain The Shadow, it's impact and influence on our lives and emotional well-being can be difficult and somewhat confusing.

I am delighted to recommend this comprehensive workbook that takes a look at all of the aspects of our being that are influenced by or even overtaken by our Shadow. There are so many avenues you can explore, so many ways of considering the Shadow and this workbook supports this experience.

Thank you very much for this excellent resource. Highly recommended by me. "

Kim, Menthal Health Coach

"Great work! Categorising the archetypes is interesting and facilitates the integration of the shadow. The questions are deep and to the point and helped me reveal more aspects of my shadow and bring them to the surface, to the light of awareness!"

Elena, Reader

"It's taught me to go from caregiver/hero to innocent. It's helped me navigate the relationship with my mum in childhood to see the repeat cycle with friends today. I have never come across one book that approaches all aspects of the shadow and covers everything! I love how practical it is. This workbook goes into Jung's theory and key words so you learn a concrete level of shadow work theory. The shadow work book delves into the archetypes and uses direct questioning to support your exploration of these characters. The trigger tracker was really useful and gave me back my power to become self aware of triggers instead of a victim to them. It was helpful to see the positives and negatives of each archetype and how we can use them. I like the tool of active imagination. Focussing on a symbol and asking questions."

Rachel, Reader

"*Writing can be an incredible act of healing. When we write, we give ourselves permission to explore our innermost thoughts and feelings, to process difficult experiences, and to find meaning in our lives. In this way, writing can be a powerful tool for personal growth and transformation.*"

SHARON SALZBERG

INTRODUCTION

I am honored to be a part of your journey towards self-discovery and growth. This is a journey that I have personally embarked upon, and one that has been transformative in my own life. It has allowed me to break free from patterns of behavior that no longer serve me and to live a more fulfilling and authentic life.

Since I started doing shadow work, I've noticed some really positive changes in my life. For one thing, I feel like I'm communicating much more effectively with the people around me. Before, I would get really easily triggered by certain things and react without thinking things through. For example, whenever someone criticized me, I would react immediately without logical thinking. This often resulted in arguments and hurt feelings, and it made it difficult for me to maintain healthy relationships. However, as I started exploring my shadow aspects, I became more aware of my triggers and learned to identify the root causes of my reactions. I discovered that my fear of rejection and my need for approval were the main sources of my trigger. By acknowledging and integrating these aspects of myself, I eventually became more emotionally resilient and less reactive. Now, when I'm triggered by something, I take a step back, breathe deeply, and try to understand the situation from a more objective perspective. This has helped me communicate more effectively and set healthier boundaries in my relationships, both personally and professionally, and I feel much more in control of my emotions.

I've also noticed that I'm making better decisions overall. Before, I would sometimes make choices based on my own biases or assumptions, without really considering all the facts or alternative perspectives. But now that I'm more aware of my own blind spots, I'm able to make more informed and thoughtful decisions that align with my values and goals. In the past, I would often agree to take on projects at work without really thinking about whether they were a good fit for me or if I had the capacity to handle them. Now that I'm more self-aware, I take the time to evaluate each opportunity carefully before committing to anything. I used to struggle with making big decisions, like choosing a career path or deciding where to live. I would often rely on others' opinions or make choices based on what I thought was expected of me. But now that I'm more in touch with my values and priorities, I'm able to make decisions that feel authentic and aligned with my true desires. I've noticed that I'm more open-minded and curious about other people's perspectives and experiences. Instead of automatically assuming that my way is the right way, I'm able to listen and learn from others, which has deepened my relationships and expanded my worldview.

Perhaps most importantly, doing shadow work has helped me gain a greater sense of purpose in my life. By confronting my own shadows, I discovered my true passion for helping others and creating positive change in the world. As I worked through my shadows, I realized that I had a deep desire to share this process with others and help them on their own journey of self-discovery. At first, the idea of publishing a workbook on shadow work was daunting; before embarking on such a journey, I first had to face my own doubts and fears around whether I was qualified to do this work and whether anyone would even be interested. But as I continued to work through my shadows, I gained the courage to take the leap and put my work out there. The process of creating this workbook has been both challenging and rewarding. On one hand, it's forced me to confront my own blind spots and biases and to really clarify my own understanding of shadow work; however, it's also given me a deep sense of purpose and fulfillment. Knowing that my work has the potential to help others on their own journey of self-discovery is incredibly meaningful to me, and it's what drives me to continue doing this work.

With every day that passes, we are constantly met with a wide range of experiences, some of which are bad, while others we may perceive as good. These experiences naturally leave a mark on our psyche, in the same way that our bodies get etched and shaped by the environment we live in. This is why it is important — necessary even — to dedicate time to care for our minds: this is what constitutes self-care.

The idea of a shadow is that it is always present behind us, yet we cannot see it in direct light. In psychological terms, the shadow refers to the parts of ourselves that we are unable to see. It became clear to me how important it is to understand our shadows when I wrote a biography of a spiritual teacher. Many of us go to great lengths to protect our self-image from anything that may be unflattering or unfamiliar. It can be easier to recognize another person's shadow before acknowledging our own. By observing the shadow of this teacher, I saw how someone can exhibit positive traits in one area of life while remaining unaware of negative behavior in other areas. This applies to all individuals. Although exploring our shadows can be both challenging and rewarding, it can lead to greater authenticity, creativity, energy, and personal growth. This introspective process is essential for reaching mature adulthood, a state that is rarer than people may realize.

The primary goal of shadow work is to confront and integrate these suppressed aspects of yourself, which can include negative patterns of behavior or thought, feelings of shame or guilt, and unresolved trauma from your past. By doing this, you can become more whole, emotionally and psychologically healthy, and less prone to self-sabotage or destructive behaviors.

Engaging in shadow work may seem daunting, but the rewards are plentiful. The process can bring about a number of positive changes in your life — one major benefit is increased self-awareness. By examining your shadow aspects with honesty and without judgment, you can become more aware of how your thoughts, emotions and behaviors impact your life. Another benefit is greater emotional resilience. Facing and integrating your shadow selves can help you become more emotionally resilient. You learn to tolerate discomfort and uncertainty, and develop a greater sense of self-acceptance, which can help you overcome setbacks and challenges. Shadow work can also improve your relationships. As you better understand and empathize with others, you can communicate more effectively and set boundaries more confidently. Additionally, embracing your shadow selves can unlock your creativity. You'll be more comfortable exploring new ideas and taking creative risks, which can lead to greater self-expression and fulfillment. These are just a few of the many positive changes that can come from engaging in the challenging, yet rewarding, process of shadow work.

This workbook is designed to guide you through the process in a safe and supportive way. It includes exercises, prompts, and reflections to help you explore your shadows and gain a deeper understanding of yourself.

I'll be honest with you and tell you that some shadow work exercises may not be easy — at least, not as easy as some people would claim — as it will involve unearthing areas of yourself you would have preferred left buried and confronting them face to face. You might start to feel uneasy or grow anxious, but don't worry as it's a natural part of the process. In fact, it might seem a bit ironic but the most effective way to avoid an emotional breakdown in any kind of therapeutic work is to stop trying to avoid it. When we try to avoid an emotional breakdown, we're more attached to having one; since we're more attached to it and resist it at the same time, our anxiety about having one then doubles. Therefore, instead of trying to avoid having an emotional breakdown, it's better to shift our attention to reality as it already exists: the facts about what has happened to us and the unresolved emotional charge in our memories of what happened. The emotional charge wants to be resolved. The emotions associated with our memories aren't the problem — our resistance to feeling them is the problem, especially when we want to deal with those memories without feeling sadness, anger or fear. However, it is impossible to process memories in the shadow of our mind without feeling strong emotions.

Our fear of feeling them is what prevents us from recovering from those harmful experiences. Attending to unresolved emotionally charged memories, feeling the emotions, and allowing them to finally resolve is hard work. It's kind of like doing a high-dive the first time and surviving it. As soon as we recognize that we survived, we feel relieved and even exhilarated. Here's the thing: we didn't wait for our fear of jumping to go away before we jumped. We felt the fear and jumped anyway.

The key to shadow work is to stay open-minded and non-judgmental as you explore your inner landscape. One way to do this is by practicing mindfulness, which involves being present and observing our thoughts and emotions without getting caught up in them or judging them. This can be incredibly helpful during this process, as it allows us to observe our shadows without becoming overwhelmed or defensive. Another way to approach shadow work with compassion is by cultivating self-compassion. This involves treating ourselves with kindness, understanding and acceptance, even when we confront our shadows. It can be easy to judge ourselves harshly during this process, but self-compassion can help us approach our shadows with greater acceptance and empathy. Using neutral language can also be helpful when describing our shadows. Rather than labeling them as "good" or "bad," we can describe them objectively using terms like "fear," "anger," or "sadness." This helps us approach things without getting caught up in judgment or moralizing. Practicing empathy with ourselves is another important aspect of this work. By putting ourselves in another person's shoes and trying to understand their perspective, we can approach our shadows with greater understanding and acceptance. It's helpful to imagine what it would be like to experience our shadows from another person's perspective.

Diving into your dark side is a challenging and sensitive process, and creating a warm and welcoming environment can make a significant difference in how successful and productive the practice is. Overall, it helps to create a sense of safety and comfort that is necessary for exploring the darker aspects of the psyche. The goal of creating a cozy environment is to create a space that is conducive to relaxation and introspection. This can include things like soft lighting, candles, comfortable seating, and calming music. These elements help to calm the nervous system and create a sense of safety, which allows you to focus on the work at hand without feeling overwhelmed or triggered.

A warm and welcoming environment can also help to cultivate a sense of self-compassion and acceptance, which is crucial when working with the shadow self. When we create a nurturing and supportive environment for ourselves, we are better equipped to confront and process the difficult emotions and memories that arise during shadow work. It can be comforting to have familiar items around us, such as blankets, pillows, or a journal, to help us ground ourselves and feel more connected to our inner experience. In addition, a nurturing environment can also help to build a sense of ritual and intention around the shadow work practice. By intentionally setting up the space, we are signaling to ourselves that this is a sacred and important time for self-discovery and growth. This can increase our motivation and commitment to the practice and help us to approach it with a more open and curious mindset.

It can be frustrating and disheartening when you've been doing shadow work for years and feel like you still haven't fully encountered your own. I know this firsthand, as I've been on this journey for a while now. However, it's important to remember that the shadow is not a static thing that can be fully discovered and then put away. It's a dynamic and constantly evolving aspect of ourselves that requires ongoing exploration and integration. It's also possible that there may be deeper layers to your shadow that you haven't yet uncovered. This can happen when we become comfortable with exploring certain aspects of ourselves but avoid the more challenging or uncomfortable parts. It's important to continue to approach shadow work with openness and curiosity, even when it feels difficult or scary. It's also worth considering whether you might be resisting the integration of certain aspects of the process. This can happen when we're attached to certain beliefs or self-images and are afraid to let them go. It's important to be gentle with yourself and to approach the process of integration with self-compassion.

If you're new to shadow work, it's a good idea to start slowly. For example, you could begin by exploring your emotions and feelings around a particular issue or challenge in your life; this could be something as simple as a fear or anxiety that you have been avoiding. It's also important to keep in mind that this process is ongoing, and you're unlikely to fully integrate your shadow aspects in a single session or even a few months. Embrace the journey. Embrace the ups and downs, and be patient and kind with yourself along the way.

Shadow work is a journey, not a destination.

So, I welcome you once again to this guide where we'll work together to ensure that you move beyond negativity, grow, and eventually reach your fullest potential.

This is my very first editorial project, and I would absolutely love to hear your constructive feedback. Feel free to reach out to me at **hello@booksquarepublishing.com**. I've poured my heart and soul into creating this workbook, hoping that it truly serves its purpose and brings value to your life. If you find it helpful in any way, I would greatly appreciate it if you could share your opinion on Amazon.

THE SHADOW

I must state at this point that this woorbook will use quite a bit of technical psychoanalytic terms as well as delve into the mechanics of your psyche, but don't you worry, I'll break it down and explain everything to you in every step of the way. After all, the importance of understanding yourself and how your mind works, what drives you and how parts of your mind operate cannot be overstated.

The Chinese military general and philosopher Sun Tzu, in his work "The Art of War" even had this to say about the essence of self-awareness and understanding: "If you know the enemy and know yourself, you need not fear the result of a hundred battles. If you know yourself but not the enemy, for every victory gained you will also suffer a defeat. If you know neither the enemy nor yourself, you will succumb in every battle."

In fact, you know what? Just think of this workbook as also a crash course on psychoanalysis. Pretty neat, right? This will allow us to kill two birds with one stone. Anyway, let's begin to explore the various concepts and how they relate to your shadow, its growth and eventual integration.

THE BIRTH OF THE SHADOW

I would like to begin by defining some important concepts that will help us throughout this journey. Firstly, I would like to differentiate between the ego-syntonic and the ego-dystonic — like I said, these things are important in understanding yourself and becoming a better person. Moreover, a little more knowledge can't hurt. So, in psychoanalysis, ego-syntonic here describes all the values, characters and behaviors that are in accord with our ideal self-image. So, let's assume you think of yourself as a fighter, you know the characteristics of fighters, their traits, and feelings, and when you look at yourself in the mirror, you find that the behaviors you display are consistent with the idea you have of yourself as a fighter. When that happens, we say that those qualities are ego-syntonic with your ego (or self). The ego-dystonic, however, is the reverse case. Any desire, idea or behavior that is clashing with your ideal self-image or what you feel are your needs and goals, is summed up as ego-dystonic. To use the fighter example once again, if, upon looking inward, you realize that none of your behaviors are in line with what you view as your ideal, then you're left with a series of ego-dystonic characters.

The shadow, as developed by the psychoanalyst, Carl Jung, is regarded as the blind spot of your psyche. Over the years, it has assumed different names such as the repressed id, the shadow aspect, the shadow archetype, and even the ego-dystonic complex (now you see why it can be called ego-dystonic). The notion of the shadow envelops the totality of things beyond the bright light of our consciousness, whether they be positive or negative. The general consensus on the matter of shadows is that it is only limited to the negative traits we are too scared to face, but that is far from true. Some positive qualities may also be buried and forgotten within our shadows — this happens especially in people with low self-esteem, anxieties, and false beliefs — and integrating with them is necessary for becoming a healthy whole.

Now, the idea of a shadow is linked intricately with that of the persona, so I'll have to briefly explain what the persona is.

Working to conceal our true nature, the Persona acts as the camouflage, a sort of cloak, we bring forward and present to the external social world. It represents all of the various social masks that we wear on a regular basis among the different people and situations we find ourselves in.

Jung warned that our complete dependence on the persona could lead to a situation where people could no longer see themselves beyond the expectations of society for them. He stated that "the danger is that [people] become identical with their personas—the professor with his textbook, the tenor with his voice." A shallow unthinking being emerges as a result, and all they become are personas, nothing more than the masks they wear. Usually, the decomposition of the persona is sought after during psychotherapy since it allows the individual's inner self to issue forth and all the excessive commitments to collective ideals are discarded — what Jung termed 'individuation' now begins to take place.

Jung theorized that our shadow self was a counterweight to our persona. Our shadow arose at the same moment your persona was born, and both had to be surpassed and integrated before one could become their true selves. Let me explain briefly how the shadow is born.

As our civilization evolved over the years and we began to interact with each other more and more, the notion of morality, that sense of right and wrong that sought to guide us, began to form, and take roots in our minds. Following the development of larger social communities as the centuries passed, we found it necessary to suppress some parts of ourselves and replace our basic desires with the interests of the common good. Everything was now at stake; our overall survival as a civilization now relied on how well we could cooperate with one another.

Now, let's fast forward to our time. How is the shadow formed? Well, it generally forms during childhood, first as a result of our natural ego development, and through the process of socialization. It is important to know that it is the process of learning how to live in a way acceptable to one's own society, which is especially true when talking about children.

As children, we show a wide range of emotions and behaviors like love, anger, generosity, selfishness, etc. But when we express these shades of ourselves growing up, we are immediately corrected, receive negative cues from our environment, and forced to modify our behaviors in order to preserve our basic needs. Generally, we depend on our parent figures for survival and as a result, develop an attachment to them. Any disapproval from your parent figure will be viewed as a threat to your safety, to the love you seek to gain and preserve, and your need to belong. As you grow older, your attention shifts from only your parent figure to also include other figures such as your friends, teachers, family members, bosses, partners, etc., and the adjustment continues.

So, when you do something they don't agree with and are scolded, you start to reject those parts of your psyche, and instead adopt a role — or if you will, a mask — that will ensure your survival both physically and psychologically. We start to learn the things society treats as bad and the things regarded as good and begin the process of dividing ourselves into numerous parts, so that we can sort out the qualities that society deems unacceptable and those that are acceptable. Some have even likened the instance of learning with the biblical eating from the tree of good and evil.

This marks the birth of the Persona, and at the same time, the birth of the Shadow. The Persona presents itself as the friendly face we show to the people around us, the part that fits in and follows the rules, while the Shadow now contains all the repressed desires we have locked away and thrown away the key. They are inseparable. But funny enough, those parts don't just disappear. Oh no, no, far from it. They continue to live on in the unconscious and assert themselves through several indirect means.

THE REPRESSION

Now, we cannot talk about shadows without discussing repression. It is after all the instrument, the medium, by which shadows take form. So, what exactly is repression? In psychoanalysis, according to the Wikipedia article, repression is defined as a defense mechanism that "ensures that what is unacceptable to the conscious mind, and would if recalled arouse anxiety, is prevented from entering into it." So, anything the mind feels is wrong, anything it can't deal with or bear, it represses or pushes away into the unconscious.

Now, as I had explained before, the process of socialization in our civilized world forces us to repress aspects of ourselves that do not fit in with the highly organized structure of our society.

However, this repression robs us of something vital. We are born whole and complete, but we slowly learn to live fractioned lives, accepting some parts of our nature but rejecting and ignoring other parts.

This acts as an enormous barrier in our ability to develop self-love and live authentically. How can you completely and whole-heartedly accept who you cannot look at certain parts of yourself, when you're too terrified to examine yourself in-depth? This is why shadow work is essential for us. But beyond the repression caused by society's education and correction on matters regarding characters that are permitted and those that aren't, the motivational teachings found all across the internet serve to proliferate the internal repression. By focusing on the light, on the good aspects of ourselves, they make us ignore the dark parts that constitute us as well. It becomes a form of escapism: a way of ignoring the responsibilities over our lives and the choices we make.

The repression of our inner shadows can lead to troubling and sometimes dire consequences, since the parts that make up our shadow self long to be heard. When we fail to acknowledge or integrate them, they find ways — sometimes subtle, sometimes overt — to manifest themselves in our lives. An important literary example and one that has found much attention in the eyes of most psychoanalysts and shadow work guides is The Strange Case of Dr. Jekyll and Mr. Hyde. In the story, the good doctor discovered a way to separate his inner dark passions from his good side with the help of a drug. As the months go by, his more corrupt side assumes more control until it overcomes him completely.

The more you evade contact with your shadow, the more difficult it will be to access. The more we avert our gaze from our darkness, the more it grows, taking roots within us like an ivy, until it springs out without warning. Some of the issues that can arise when we reject our Shadow side include:

CONSTANTLY SABOTAGING ONESELF: This could manifest in a variety of ways, such as consistently procrastinating on important tasks, self-medicating with drugs or alcohol, engaging in self-destructive behaviors like overspending or gambling, or constantly putting oneself down and believing that failure is inevitable.

AN UNHEALTHY HABIT OF MANIPULATING OTHERS: This could involve manipulating others for personal gain or to maintain control over a situation. For example, someone might use emotional blackmail to get what they want from others, or they might lie or deceive to get ahead in their career.

A SENSE OF SELF-LOATHING: This could manifest in negative self-talk, believing that one is worthless or undeserving of love or success, or engaging in self-harming behaviors such as cutting or burning oneself.

AN INFLATED EGO, BORDERING ON NARCISSISM: This could involve an excessive preoccupation with one's own achievements, talents or appearance, and a lack of empathy or consideration for others. For example, someone might constantly talk about their accomplishments and belittle others' achievements, or they might expect special treatment and entitlement.

HYPOCRISY IN THE WAY ONE LIVES: This could involve preaching one thing but practicing another, or having a public persona that is vastly different from one's private behavior. For example, someone might promote healthy living but secretly engage in unhealthy behaviors themselves, or they might claim to value honesty but lie frequently.

A CRIPPLING LOW SENSE OF SELF-WORTH AND SELF-ESTEEM: This could manifest in a variety of ways, such as feeling undeserving of love or success, constantly seeking validation and approval from others, or engaging in self-sabotaging behaviors to reinforce negative beliefs about oneself.

DEPRESSION, WHICH MOST TIMES OFTEN EVOLVES INTO SUICIDAL TENDENCIES: Depression can be characterized by persistent feelings of sadness, hopelessness and worthlessness, as well as a lack of interest in activities that one used to enjoy. In severe cases, depression can lead to suicidal ideation or attempts, which require immediate medical attention.

A very important psychological phenomenon that occurs as a result of repression is something called projection. Projection describes the tendency of seeing things in others that are in fact within us — it is generally traits we consciously avoid and deny.

For example, if you grew up being told that being confident was wrong by your parents or guardians, and you later find someone who is acting confident around you, an irritation might start to build up. The confidence you had repressed as a result of perceiving it as a negative quality as well as its associated negative emotional affect or load now becomes projected onto other people. This process of projection is an unconscious one that hides beyond the reach of our awareness. It is a defense mechanism meant to protect our distorted sense of self-image, thus creating a divide between the image and our actual self — a sort of hypocrisy sets in.

Now, those who are caught in our web of projection suffer many kinds of punishment, be it harsh criticism, rejection, some form of physical or verbal abuse, etc., and this has the effect of causing chaotic dysfunctional relationships with others.

So, in order to move forward, we have to overcome these projections. We have to retrieve and reclaim them from the depths of our unconscious through shadow work.

THE IMPORTANCE OF INTEGRATION

Integration refers to the process of acknowledging and accepting the different aspects of oneself, including those that may be uncomfortable or unpleasant. This involves recognizing and accepting the shadow, which is the part of oneself that contains aspects that are repressed or denied. Through integration, one seeks to understand and make peace with the shadow, integrating it into one's sense of self. This allows for a more complete understanding of oneself and promotes personal growth.

The majority of people who wish to growth spiritually are fond of using spirituality as an excuse for hiding away from their otherwise unseemly aspect, and this prevents them from achieving true spiritual awakening and wholeness (as the word 'integration' would imply, since it literally means to make whole from parts). They seek to bypass their darkness spiritually, instead of owning it. What is the opposite of integration? Differentiation — a fragmentation of something into bits. There is a complete breakdown, total eventual disintegration of the person's psychological composure. Everything that had been previously repressed comes pouring out with an explosive force.

Therefore, integration is essential for personal growth and well-being. It involves developing the ability to understand others better and possessing a greater sense of compassion towards them. By integrating different perspectives and experiences, you gain a broader understanding of the world and the people around you. This leads to a form of inner tranquility, allowing you to feel more at peace with yourself and those around you. Furthermore, integration can lead to self-healing by helping you to reconcile different parts of yourself and your past. By acknowledging and integrating past traumas, you can move forward in a healthier way, free from the emotional baggage that may have previously held you back. Additionally, integration allows you to develop the ability to appropriately respond to the problems life throws at you, rather than simply reacting to them without any proper awareness.

Integration and embracing the shadow are two concepts that are often used in same context. However, while they share similarities, they are not the same: integration involves acknowledging and accepting the shadow, while embracing the shadow involves actively exploring and engaging with it. Both concepts are valuable for personal growth and self-improvement, but they differ in their level of engagement with the shadow.

EMBRACING THE SHADOW

Embracing the shadow, on the other hand, goes a step further than integration. It involves actively seeking out and exploring the shadow, not just accepting it. This means facing and engaging with the uncomfortable or painful aspects of oneself, without judgment or shame. By embracing the shadow, one seeks to uncover and integrate the parts of oneself that were previously hidden, leading to greater self-awareness and personal transformation.

Though it may seem counterintuitive, recognizing and acknowledging our negative traits can help us understand ourselves better. Knowing our flaws and shortcomings can help us work on them, leading to significant personal growth.

Additionally, embracing our shadow self can help us develop empathy and understanding for others. It is all too easy to judge and condemn other people for their shortcomings without acknowledging our own. Recognizing and accepting our own negative traits can help us better understand and relate to others instead of being judgmental. Here are ways to embrace your shadow:

RECOGNIZE YOUR SHADOW SELF: The first step to embracing your shadow self is recognizing it. Take time to reflect on yourself, exploring both your positive and negative traits. Consider your deepest desires, fears, emotional triggers and negative patterns of behavior. It is important that you keep in mind that identifying and acknowledging your shadow self can be difficult, so be patient and kind to yourself as you work through it.

PRACTICE SELF-COMPASSION: Embracing your shadow self requires self-compassion and kindness. Often, we hold ourselves to an unrealistic standard, expecting perfection from ourselves. This attitude only serves to repress our shadow self and distance ourselves from our true selves. Instead, practice self-compassion, thus acknowledging that you are human and it is okay to have flaws.

EMBRACE VULNERABILITY: Embracing your shadow self requires vulnerability, which can be challenging to do. It is easy to hide our flaws and present a more polished version of ourselves to others. However, true personal growth and understanding can only come from embracing vulnerability. Share your shadow traits with trusted friends or a therapist — allow yourself to be seen and understood for who you truly are.

WORK ON YOUR FLAWS: Once you have identified your shadow traits, work on them actively. Recognize when your negative patterns of behavior emerge and take the necessary steps to correct them. Develop a system of accountability, such as working with a therapist or trusted friend, to help you stay on track.

LEARN FROM MISTAKES: Embracing your shadow self means understanding that mistakes and failures are inevitable. Instead of denying or avoiding them, learn from them. Identify what went wrong, and work on correcting and adjusting your behavior going forward.

CULTIVATE MINDFULNESS: Cultivating mindfulness can help you embrace your shadow self more easily. Mindfulness involves focusing your attention on the present moment, without judgment or criticism. Practice mindfulness meditation by focusing your attention on your breath and allowing your thoughts to flow freely. Through mindfulness, you can develop a deeper understanding of your thoughts and emotions, including your shadow self.

Embracing your shadow self is essential for personal growth and development. It can be a challenging and uncomfortable process, but one that is worth undertaking. Recognize your shadow self, practice self-compassion and vulnerability, work on your flaws, learn from mistakes, and cultivate mindfulness. By embracing your shadow self, you can develop a better understanding of yourself, empathize with others, and achieve greater personal growth. Let us go on and see what else we can learn.

RELEASING TRAUMA THROUGH SHADOW WORK

As humans, we all experience some form of trauma in our lives. Traumatic experiences can have a lasting impact on us, thereby affecting our mental, emotional and even physical well-being. Traditionally, therapy and/or medication have been recommended in order to deal with trauma, but the relatively new method that has gained popularity is shadow work.

Since shadow work involves facing parts of ourselves we normally deny or avoid, during this process, we can confront our traumas and release them. Trauma often stems from our past experiences, which have led us to develop coping and defense mechanisms to deal with pain and discomfort. However, while these mechanisms may have helped us in the moment, they can also become hindrances in our present lives, stopping us from fully experiencing our emotions and connecting with others.

By acknowledging and accepting our shadow, we can begin to heal from our traumas. We can recognize how our coping mechanisms developed and how they may be limiting us now. We can then begin to rebuild our identity by choosing new coping mechanisms and defense mechanisms that serve us better.

Shadow work also allows us to develop a deeper understanding and empathy towards ourselves and others. By confronting our own traumas, we can develop compassion for ourselves and recognize that everyone else is also dealing with their own struggles. This can help us to break down barriers and form stronger connections with others in our lives.

As a powerful tool for healing from trauma, shadow work allows us to confront and integrate our shadow, then release our traumas and develop a deeper understanding and empathy towards ourselves and others. If you're interested in exploring shadow work, consider seeking out a therapist or a trained shadow work practitioner to guide you through the process. With time, patience and dedication, you can move towards a more authentic and fulfilling life.

SHADOW WORK AND INNER CHILD HEALING: EXPLORING THE CONNECTION

In a world where we are constantly bombarded with messages telling us how to think, feel and behave, it is easy to lose touch with our true selves. Our deepest feelings and desires get buried beneath a pile of societal expectations, insecurities, and traumas, making it difficult to access our inner wisdom and navigate life with clarity and authenticity. However, by engaging in two powerful practices – Shadow Work and Inner Child Healing – we can peel back the layers of conditioning and discover our authentic selves, leading to greater self-awareness, emotional healing, and personal transformation.

The overall process aims to bring these shadows into conscious awareness, so we can understand and accept them, instead of running away from them. It involves acknowledging our fears, doubts and insecurities; it also explores where they come from, what triggers them and how they affect our behavior. By shining a light on these aspects of ourselves, we can start to dismantle the limiting beliefs and negative scripts that have been holding us back and create a more authentic and empowered version of ourselves.

What is Inner Child Healing? Inner Child Healing is a related practice that focuses on healing and nurturing the wounded parts of us that were formed in childhood. Our inner child refers to the vulnerable and sensitive aspects of our psyche that were shaped by our early experiences – both positive and negative. When we experienced love, safety and affirmation as children, our inner child was happy and thriving. But when we experienced neglect, abuse or trauma, our inner child became wounded and started to develop negative beliefs and emotional patterns that still affect us today.

Inner Child Healing aims to heal these wounds and reconnect with our inner child – the part of us that knows how to play, dream and trust. It involves revisiting and processing our past experiences, identifying, and releasing negative beliefs and emotions, and nurturing our inner child with love and acceptance. By doing so, we can create a sense of safety and security within ourselves and start to live from a place of authenticity and self-love.

Some common practices used in Inner Child Healing include inner dialogue, visualization, creative expression, and self-care rituals. These practices help us connect with our inner child on an emotional level and create a safe and loving environment where they can heal and grow. Through this healing, we can start to dismantle the negative patterns and beliefs that were formed in childhood and create a new, more empowering narrative for ourselves.

Why shadow work and inner child healing are critical for personal transformation?

When we engage in Shadow Work and Inner Child Healing, we give ourselves the gift of self-awareness and emotional healing. We learn to recognize and accept all aspects of ourselves – the good, the bad, and the ugly – then use them as sources of growth and transformation. We stop running away from our shadows and start integrating them into our wholeness, creating a more authentic and empowered version of ourselves.

Both these practices are critical for personal transformation because they allow us to address the underlying causes of our limiting beliefs and negative patterns. Instead of treating the symptoms, we go to the root of the problem and heal the wounds that created them. By doing so, we create a solid foundation for a more compassionate, fulfilling and meaningful life.

Engaging in Shadow Work and Inner Child Healing is not always easy. It requires courage, vulnerability, and a willingness to face our fears and insecurities. However, the rewards of these practices are immense — greater self-awareness, emotional healing, and personal transformation. As we learn to embrace and nurture all aspects of ourselves, we create a deeper connection with our true selves, others and the world around us.

In conclusion, shadow work focuses on uncovering and integrating the unconscious aspects of our personality, while Inner Child Healing involves addressing and healing the emotional wounds from our childhood. Both practices can be powerful tools for personal growth and transformation that can help us access our inner wisdom and transform our lives. By bringing our shadows and wounded parts into conscious awareness and offering them love and acceptance, we free ourselves from the shackles of negative beliefs and patterns and create a more authentic and fulfilling life. So, if you are ready to go on a journey of self-discovery and personal growth, consider engaging in these practices and watch as your life transforms in unimaginable ways.

WAYS TO ENCOUNTER YOUR SHADOW

Discovering your shadow self may seem challenging at first, but there are various approaches that can help you understand your shadow better.

At the same time, integrating different strategies can be a powerful way to approach your healing journey. It's important to start with self-reflection and take the time to consider what areas of your life you want to work on and what strategies might be most effective for you. Remember to honor your personality, learning style and comfort level with different techniques. Once you've identified some strategies that resonate with you, try mixing and matching them to find what works best. You might journal about your shadow aspects and then use guided meditations to explore them more deeply. Or, you might write in your journal about a particular shadow aspect, and then create a painting or drawing that represents your feelings about it. You might try attending a yoga or dance class that focuses on the chakras, and then use a guided meditation to explore any insights or emotions that come up. You might also attend a workshop or group therapy session focused on shadow work, and then continue to explore your shadows through individual practice at home.

Staying open and curious is also essential. Be open to trying new things and exploring different techniques. Keeping an open mind and staying curious about your inner world will allow you to be more receptive to new experiences and insights.

Creating a routine that incorporates different techniques is also helpful. Develop a regular routine that works best for you and your schedule. This can help you stay consistent and committed to your shadow work.

There is no one "right" way to do it. However, by effectively incorporating different strategies and techniques, you can create a customized approach that works best for you and your unique needs. Trust the process, be patient and compassionate with yourself, and know that every step you take towards self-awareness and healing is a step towards growth and transformation.

I understand that the process of shadow work can seem overwhelming, especially for someone who is new to the practice. That's why I'm happy to suggest some techniques for each archetype as a starting point. However, it's important to remember that these suggestions are just that: starting points. Ultimately, each person's journey with shadow work is unique, and it's important to allow yourself the freedom to experiment and explore at your own pace. Trusting the flow of your emotions and intuition can be a powerful way to uncover hidden aspects of yourself and promote healing and growth. So while these techniques can be helpful to get started, remember to listen to your own inner wisdom as you navigate your shadow work journey.

Caregiver: Consider the ways in which you may be sacrificing your own needs and boundaries for the sake of others. Practice setting healthy boundaries and making time for self-care.

Creator: Practice allowing yourself to make mistakes and embrace imperfection. Consider exploring any perfectionistic tendencies that may be holding you back creatively.

Everyman: Journaling can be a helpful tool for exploring your thoughts and emotions. Allow yourself to feel and express any pain or sadness you may be holding onto, and consider seeking support from a therapist or trusted friend.

Explorer: Spend time exploring your beliefs and values, and question any assumptions or biases you may hold. Practice sitting with uncertainty and embracing the unknown.

Hero: Practice sitting with discomfort and vulnerability. Allow yourself to acknowledge your fears and insecurities, and try to build a sense of inner strength and resilience.

Innocent: Try to explore the darker aspects of life and acknowledge that bad things happen in the world. Practice self-compassion and give yourself permission to feel a range of emotions, including fear and sadness.

Jester: Practice allowing yourself to feel and express a range of emotions, including sadness and vulnerability. Consider exploring any avoidance or numbing behaviors that may be preventing you from fully experiencing life.

Lover: Explore any patterns of co-dependency or attachment, and practice cultivating self-love and self-compassion. Consider working on building a strong sense of self outside of relationships.

Magician: Consider the ways in which you may be using your power or influence to manipulate others, and practice using your gifts and talents for positive change. Practice mindfulness and intention-setting.

Ruler: Consider the ways in which you may be controlling or perfectionistic, and practice letting go of the need to be in control. Practice delegating tasks and trusting others to help you.

Sage: Spend time exploring your beliefs and knowledge, and question any assumptions or biases you may hold. Practice humility and openness to new ideas and perspectives.

FLYING SOLO?

Shadow work is not a common practice, and only few people are trained in this type of psychotherapy, so it is essential to decide if you'll be approaching the process alone or with the aid of professional help.

In shadow work, it isn't necessary to seek out therapists, as it is something you can do entirely on your own, but having someone else there has its benefits. For starters, they can offer prompts that have been made specifically for you. More importantly, they can also uncover hidden patterns in your behaviors, dreams, etc., and guide you through dealing with different emotional triggers.

It's not everyone that should perform shadow work alone. For those struggling with deep trauma or mental health issues, they definitely should seek out help from a professional.

SELF-CARE

Self-care is an essential component of shadow work, as it helps to support and nurture you as you navigate difficult emotions and experiences. By taking care of yourself physically, emotionally, and spiritually, you can create a strong foundation for your inner work and help yourself to navigate challenging emotions and experiences with greater ease and resilience.

Here are some ways in which self-care can be beneficial during this journey:

- Reducing stress and anxiety: Shadow work can bring up intense emotions, which can be overwhelming at times. Practicing self-care techniques such as deep breathing, meditation or taking a relaxing bath can help to reduce stress and anxiety.

- Building self-compassion: Shadow work often involves exploring aspects of ourselves that we may feel ashamed or embarrassed about.

- Practicing self-compassion, such as treating yourself kindly, talking to yourself like you would a friend, and acknowledging your progress, can help to build resilience and self-esteem.

- Promoting physical health: Engaging in physical self-care, such as getting regular exercise, eating a healthy diet, and getting enough sleep, can help to improve your overall well-being and support you in managing any physical symptoms of stress or anxiety that may arise during shadow work.

- Creating a sense of safety: Shadow work can bring up feelings of vulnerability and fear. Practicing self-care by creating a safe and nurturing environment can help you feel more grounded and secure. This can include surrounding yourself with supportive people, establishing healthy boundaries, and engaging in activities that bring you joy and comfort.

Essential Oils

Given that essential oils are often considered an important element of self-care practices, I thought you might appreciate some recommendations on which oils might best suit your particular archetype. However, it's important to note that these are simply suggestions inspired by the archetypes and should not be construed as definitive or official essential oil blends.

Caregiver: Chamomile oil, which is calming and nurturing, and can promote a sense of compassion and care.

Creator: Bergamot oil, which is inspiring and uplifting, and can promote a sense of creativity and innovation.

Everyman: Cedarwood oil, which is comforting and reliable, and can promote a sense of stability and dependability.

Explorer: Peppermint oil, which is energizing and refreshing, and can promote a sense of adventure and exploration.

Hero: Rosemary oil, which is invigorating and stimulating, and can promote a sense of courage and strength.

Innocent: Lavender oil, which is calming and soothing, and can promote a sense of purity and innocence.

Jester: Sweet orange oil, which is playful and uplifting, and can promote a sense of humor and light-heartedness.

Lover: Ylang-ylang oil, which is sensual and romantic, and can promote a sense of passion and intimacy.

Magician: Clary sage oil, which is mystical and transformative, and can promote a sense of magic and creativity.

Outlaw: Patchouli oil, which is earthy and unconventional, and can promote a sense of rebellion and nonconformity.

Ruler: Myrrh oil, which is regal and luxurious, and can promote a sense of power and authority.

Sage: Frankincense oil, which is grounding and meditative, and can promote a sense of wisdom and introspection.

Download "Trigger Tracker and Processing" Printable

Dismantling triggers involves a little detective work and it isn't always easy to do it on your own, especially if you are new at shadow work. For this reason, I put together a special trigger log that provides a structured way to track your emotional responses and gain insight into your underlying psychological patterns. By tracking and processing these triggers, you can begin to identify patterns and gain insight into the underlying issues that may be driving your negative emotions or behaviors. Once these triggers have been identified, you can then begin the process of working through your shadow issues. This may involve exploring past experiences or traumas, examining core beliefs and values, or engaging in therapeutic practices such as journaling or meditation.

To download your printable PDF, simply scan the QR code.

You'll also get a printable version of the **Guided Journal** within the same file!

Explore the Guided Journal, which is located at the end of this workbook, and feel free to print and reuse your favorite pages as often as you'd like.

IDENTIFY YOUR TRIGGERS

Knowing the kind of situations that bring out your shadow is a step that shouldn't be omitted. During what sort of events does your anger, anxiety, fear or shame manifest itself?

To identify your triggers during shadow work, think about past situations that have caused you to feel strong emotions such as anger, fear, shame or guilt. Ask yourself what specifically triggered those emotions and try to identify any underlying beliefs or values that were challenged.

You can also pay attention to your body's physical reactions, such as increased heart rate or tension in certain areas. These physical reactions can be a signal that something is triggering you.

Ask trusted friends or family members if they have noticed any patterns in your behavior or reactions to certain situations. Sometimes, others can see things about us that we are blind to.

Another helpful approach is to pay attention to recurring patterns or themes in your life. Notice if there are certain situations or people that seem to consistently evoke a strong emotional response from you. These patterns can help you identify your triggers and explore the underlying shadow aspects that may be at play.

By identifying your triggers and exploring the emotions and shadow aspects they bring up, you can gain deeper insight into your unconscious patterns and work towards integrating your shadow self. Again, write them down. Your journal is one of your most indispensable tools in your journey, and it will allow you to analyze yourself even later in the future. Like I said, you aren't going to answer all the questions in a single day, so it really helps to have a journal. Repeating themes should be sought for among the majority of thoughts penned down.

How to create a personalized trigger log in your journal:

By following the steps below, you can create a detailed and personalized trigger log that can help you better understand yourself and develop healthy coping mechanisms.

1. Choose a specific trigger: When selecting a trigger, it can be helpful to focus on something that frequently causes you to experience strong emotions or reactions. This could be a particular person, a specific situation, a recurring thought pattern, or anything else that consistently affects you.

2. Record the trigger: Write down the trigger in your journal, using as much detail as possible. This could include the who, what, when, where, and why of the trigger, as well as any other relevant information.

3. Note your reactions: When you encounter the trigger, pay attention to your initial reactions. Write down how you feel, any physical sensations you experience, and any thoughts that come to mind.

4. Analyze the trigger: Take some time to reflect on why the trigger affects you the way it does; Write down any insights you gain from this reflection. Ask yourself questions like:

    What is it about this trigger that makes me feel this way?

    Are there any past experiences that are contributing to my reaction?

    Do I have any underlying fears or insecurities that are being triggered?

5. Identify coping strategies: Think about healthy ways you can respond to the trigger when it arises. This could include things like deep breathing, positive self-talk, meditation, or seeking support from a friend or therapist. Write down a few coping strategies that you think could be helpful.

6. Track your progress: Over time, keep a record of how you respond to the trigger and which coping strategies you use. Reflect on whether your reactions are changing, and whether your coping strategies are effective. Use this information to adjust your approach as needed.

JOURNALING

Keeping a journal is an excellent way to gain insight into our thoughts and emotions. Writing allows us to express the parts of ourselves that we may not feel comfortable sharing with others or even acknowledging within ourselves. It can also be cathartic as it can serve as a release for the emotions and feelings that we've been carrying around. By writing about our pain or struggles, we can find a sense of relief and closure. It can be a way to process our emotions and let go of negative patterns of thinking that may be holding us back, without us even realizing it.

Daily journaling, freely expressed without any limitations in place, gives you the opportunity to pour out your emotions, as well as analyze your thoughts. Your experiences and the desires associated or born from them now have a chance to escape uncensored, and with that, you can then explore yourself even more. It is important to look for themes in your writings as this will offer insight into your unconscious mind.

The first step is to set aside some time each day to write in your journal. It is important to prioritize this time so that you can be consistent with your practice. Once you have established this habit, you can begin to write down any negative thoughts or emotions that come up for you throughout the day. This can be anything that causes you distress, such as fear, anxiety or sadness.

After you have written down your negative thoughts and emotions, take some time to reflect on why they are coming up for you. Is there a deeper fear or insecurity that is driving these feelings? It can be helpful to explore these feelings and try to understand where they are coming from.

Next, try to identify any patterns in your negative thoughts and emotions. Do they tend to come up in certain situations or with certain people? Once you have identified some patterns, think about where they may have originated. Did you have a past experience that may be influencing your current thoughts and emotions?

Finally, write down some affirmations or positive statements to counteract these negative thoughts and emotions. For example, if you are struggling with feelings of unworthiness, you could write down affirmations such as "I am worthy of love and respect" or "I am enough just as I am." By focusing on positive statements, you can begin to rewire your thought patterns and create a more positive outlook on life. With regular practice, journaling can be a powerful tool for self-reflection and personal growth.

MEDITATION

By engaging in meditation, you begin to observe yourself objectively; you start to feel and analyze your emotions better. All the triggers that usually surface to cause anxiety and other unpleasant emotional reactions become better understood.

During this moment, it can also be helpful for you to think back to your childhood and all the memories that might have had a hand in causing your repression and creating your triggers in their wake. Even the seemingly trivial might have had profound consequences on your life, so leave no stone unturned.

While there are no specific meditation practices that are exclusive to any archetype, certain types of meditation can help support different aspects of each archetype. Here are some meditation practices that may be beneficial for each archetype:

Caregiver: Self-compassion meditation to cultivate self-love and care.

Creator: Mindfulness meditation to focus on the present moment and enhance creativity.

Everyman: Mindful walking meditation to increase awareness and connection with the environment.

Explorer: Visualization meditation to explore new perspectives and possibilities.

Hero: Mantra meditation to cultivate inner strength and resilience.

Innocent: Breath awareness meditation to promote relaxation and calmness.

Jester: Laughter meditation to release tension and promote joy.

Lover: Heart-centered meditation to promote emotional openness and connection.

Magician: Transcendental meditation to access higher states of consciousness and creativity.

Outlaw: Mindful breathing meditation to develop self-awareness and regulate emotions.

Ruler: Loving-kindness meditation to cultivate compassion and empathy for oneself and others.

Sage: Insight meditation to develop wisdom and insight.

TEA MEDITATION

Tea meditation is a practice of mindfulness that involves focusing on the present moment while drinking a cup of tea. It can be a useful tool during shadow work as it can help to create a safe and calm space for self-reflection and self-discovery.

During tea meditation, you can create a ritual of making and drinking tea, which can be a soothing and comforting experience. As you drink your tea, you can focus on the sensations and tastes in your mouth, and the warmth and aroma of the tea. This can help you to stay present in the moment and connect with your body, which can be grounding during times of emotional turmoil.

You can also use the tea meditation practice to reflect on your thoughts and emotions as they arise during shadow work. By observing them without judgment or attachment, you can gain a deeper understanding of your inner world and the parts of yourself that you may be avoiding or suppressing.

I thought you may find it helpful to receive suggestions on which tea blends to use based on your archetype.

Caregiver: A nurturing and comforting blend of chamomile, elderflower, and lemon balm.

Creator: A creative and imaginative blend of green tea, jasmine flowers, and passionfruit.

Everyman: A classic and reliable blend of English breakfast tea and milk.

Explorer: A spicy and adventurous blend of black tea, ginger, and cinnamon.

Hero: A bold and energizing blend of yerba mate, peppermint, and citrus.

Innocent: A simple and pure blend of white tea and chamomile flowers.

Jester: A playful and humorous blend of fruit tea, such as strawberry and kiwi.

Lover: A sensual and romantic blend of rose petals, hibiscus, and honeybush tea.

Magician: A mystical and transformative blend of pu-erh tea, chai spices, and goji berries.

Outlaw: A rebellious and unconventional blend of black tea, bergamot, and vanilla.

Ruler: A regal and luxurious blend of white tea, bergamot, and rosemary.

Sage: A calming and introspective blend of green tea, mint, and lavender.

Please note that these are just ideas and not necessarily based on any scientific or traditional associations. These recommendations are merely suggestions inspired by the archetypes.

AFFIRMATIONS

Using affirmations during shadow work can be a powerful tool for transformation and growth. Affirmations are positive statements that can help reprogram your subconscious mind and shift your beliefs and thought patterns. They can help you counteract negative self-talk and replace it with more empowering and uplifting messages.

Start by identifying the negative beliefs or self-talk that come up during your shadow work. For example, you might notice thoughts like "I'm not good enough" or "I don't deserve love." Then, create a positive affirmation that directly counters that belief or pattern. For example, you might create an affirmation like "I am worthy and deserving of love and acceptance."

Repeat your affirmations daily, either silently or out loud, and try to really feel the truth of the statement. It can also be helpful to write your affirmations down or place them somewhere visible, like on a sticky note or as a phone background, to remind you throughout the day.

Visualize yourself embodying the positive qualities in your affirmations. When you repeat your them, try to really feel the truth of the statements then imagine what it would be like to fully embody those qualities in your life.

ANALYZING YOUR DREAMS

Jung and Freud both agreed that dreams were invaluable devices in exploring and understanding the unconscious.

To begin analyzing your dreams, keep a dream journal and record your dreams as soon as you wake up, before the details fade away. Look for common themes, symbols and emotions that appear in your dreams. You can also try to identify any connections between your dreams and actual events or experiences in your waking life. By studying the patterns recurring throughout the dreams as you log them in your journal, you begin to notice certain otherwise concealed parts of yourself.

One way to interpret your dreams is through a process called amplification, where you explore the significance of a symbol or image by associating it with various cultural, historical or personal meanings. You can also use active imagination, a technique developed by Carl Jung, to engage with the images and characters in your dreams by visualizing and dialoguing with them.

It's important to approach dream analysis with an open and curious mindset, rather than trying to force a specific interpretation. Dreams can be complex and multilayered, and their meanings may change over time. Working with a therapist or counselor who specializes in dream analysis can also be helpful in gaining deeper insights into your dreams and their potential relevance to your life.

SHADOW COMMUNICATION

Your shadow is an important aspect of your psyche that often goes unheard. But by starting a conversation with it, you can unlock a wealth of knowledge and understanding about yourself. Don't be afraid to ask your shadow tough questions and listen closely to its responses, even if they might be uncomfortable or unfamiliar.

How will my shadow respond? It could be through a sudden insight or realization, a dream, a strong emotion, a memory resurfacing, or even through physical sensations in the body. The answers may come in different forms and at different times, so it's important to remain open and patient during the process of engaging with the shadow; it is also important to approach the conversation without judgment or preconceived notions. Remember, your shadow is a part of you, and by embracing and integrating it, you can become a more whole and authentic person. So start that inner dialogue and see where the journey takes you. Here you have some questions that can get you started:

What am I avoiding or denying about myself?

What parts of myself do I fear or reject?

What aspects of myself am I ashamed of?

What patterns or behaviors do I consistently engage in that hold me back?

What limiting beliefs or negative self-talk do I have?

What childhood experiences have shaped my shadow and how does it affect me today?

What unhealed wounds or traumas am I carrying and how do they show up in my life?

How can I integrate and embrace my shadow aspects to become a more whole and authentic version of myself?

How can I use my shadow to achieve my goals and live a more fulfilling life?

How can I show more compassion and forgiveness to myself and others?

What are some of my deepest fears and insecurities, and how have they held me back in my life?

Are there any patterns or behaviors in my life that I'm not aware of, but are causing harm to myself or others?

What are some of my greatest strengths and passions, and how can I tap into them more fully?

Is there anything from my past that is still impacting me in the present, and how can I release it?

What are some limiting beliefs I hold about myself or the world, and how can I challenge and transform them?

ACTIVE IMAGINATION

This is a technique developed by Carl Jung to explore the unconscious mind. It involves using visualization and imagination to engage in a dialogue with the unconscious, which can reveal valuable insights into the hidden aspects of ourselves.

To practice active imagination, find a quiet and comfortable space where you won't be disturbed. Start by closing your eyes and taking a few deep breaths to relax your body and mind. Then, begin to visualize a symbol or archetype that has personal meaning for you. This could be anything from a tree, bird, dragon; it could even be a mere color or shape.

Once you have the symbol in mind, begin to engage with it in a dialogue. Ask it questions, listen to its responses and allow the conversation to flow naturally. Don't try to control the dialogue or force it in any particular direction — simply let it unfold as it will.

For example, if you visualize a dark figure, you might ask it, "Who are you? What do you represent in my unconscious mind? Why have you appeared in my mind at this moment? What message do you have for me? What do you want me to know about myself or my situation? How can I integrate your message into my life?" and then listen to its response. You might be surprised at what comes up: the figure could represent a repressed emotion, forgotten memory or a part of yourself that you've been hiding from.

As you continue to practice active imagination, you may find that you're able to access deeper layers of the unconscious and gain a greater understanding of yourself and your inner world.

SELF-REFLECTION

Taking time for self-reflection is an essential part of shadow work. It requires you to examine yourself honestly and without judgment. By reflecting on your beliefs, values and behaviors, you can gain a better understanding of yourself and the unconscious patterns that may be holding you back. Start by asking yourself why you hold certain beliefs and values. Are they truly your own, or have they been imposed on you by others? Are they still relevant and aligned with your authentic self or do they no longer serve you? Be honest with yourself and allow yourself to challenge any beliefs or values that don't feel true to you. It's also important to identify any behaviors or habits that you may be ashamed of or avoid. These may be indicators of shadow aspects that you have been repressing. Explore the underlying reasons for these behaviors or habits.

Identifying them can be challenging, but there are some strategies that can help. Start by paying attention to your thoughts and emotions when you find yourself engaging in certain behaviors or habits. Do you feel guilty or ashamed? Do you feel like you're not living up to your own expectations or values? These can be clues that the behavior or habit is something that you're avoiding or that is causing you shame. You can also try journaling about your thoughts and feelings related to these behaviors or habits. Write down your experiences and explore the underlying reasons for why you engage in them. Are they related to past experiences or traumas? Are they a way of coping with stress or anxiety? Reflecting on these questions can help you gain greater self-awareness and insight into your behaviors and habits. Another strategy is to seek feedback from trusted friends or family members. Ask them for their honest opinion about your behaviors and habits and listen to their feedback without getting defensive. This can be a helpful way to gain an outside perspective on your behaviors and habits.

By understanding the root causes of these behaviors, you can begin to integrate and heal these shadow aspects.

SHADOW WORK EXERCISES

There are several shadow-work exercises that you can try, such as the Empty Chair exercise, where you sit across an empty chair and imagine a person or situation that triggers a negative emotion in you. You can then express your feelings to the empty chair as if you were speaking to the person or situation. It is a powerful tool for shadow work because involves working with the unconscious aspects of your psyche that have been repressed or denied. By giving voice to your emotions and allowing yourself to express them in a safe and controlled way, you can begin to integrate these parts of yourself and move towards a greater sense of wholeness and self-awareness.

Empty Chair

The Empty Chair can be particularly helpful for working through issues related to relationships or past experiences that may be triggering negative emotions. By speaking directly to the empty chair, we are essentially speaking to the person or situation that has caused us harm or pain, and allowing ourselves to fully express and process those emotions in a safe and controlled environment. It can also be seen as a form of visualization, where we are using our imagination and senses to create a more vivid and tangible experience. This can help to activate different parts of our brain and facilitate a deeper level of emotional processing. Here's how you can practice it:

1. Find a quiet space where you won't be disturbed. Sit facing an empty chair and imagine that the person or situation that triggers negative emotions in you is sitting in that chair.

2. Allow yourself to feel the emotions that come up as you visualize this person or situation. Make a mental note of any sensations in your body, any thoughts or beliefs that arise and any emotions that you feel.

3. Begin to speak to the empty chair as if the person or situation were actually there. Express your feelings honestly and openly, without holding back. You might want to say things like, "I feel hurt and angry when you treat me that way" or "I'm afraid of being rejected by you."

4. Allow the empty chair to respond, either by imagining what the person might say or by speaking for them out loud. You might be surprised by what comes up when you allow yourself to speak and listen in this way.

5. Continue the conversation as long as you need to, until you feel a sense of resolution or closure. You might want to end the conversation by thanking the empty chair (and the person or situation it represents) for helping you to gain clarity and insight.

The Mirror

Another common self-reflection technique used in personal growth and self-improvement is The Mirror exercise. It involves looking into a mirror and examining your thoughts and feelings about yourself. Here's an explanation of this exercise from a psychological perspective: It is based on the idea that we are often influenced by how we perceive ourselves and how we think others perceive us. When we look at ourselves in the mirror, we are confronted with an image that is often different from the one we hold in our minds. This can cause feelings of discomfort or even shock.

Through this exercise, we can start to examine the thoughts and beliefs that underlie our self-perception. For example, if we notice that we have negative thoughts about our appearance, we can begin to question where these thoughts come from and how they are impacting our self-esteem. We can also examine the emotions that come up as we look at ourselves, such as shame or embarrassment.

By bringing these thoughts and emotions to the surface, we can begin to challenge them and develop a more positive and realistic sense of self. This can lead to greater self-awareness and self-acceptance, which can have positive effects on our mental health and well-being. Here's how you can practice it:

1. Find a quiet and private space where you can be alone.

2. Stand in front of a full-length mirror and look at yourself.

3. Take a deep breath and ask yourself, "What is it about myself that I don't want to face or accept?"

4. Listen to your thoughts and feelings as they come up. Be honest with yourself and don't judge what you see or feel.

5. Repeat the question, "What is it about myself that I don't want to face or accept?" and continue to listen to your thoughts and feelings.

6. When you feel ready, try to express your feelings out loud. This can be difficult, so be patient and gentle with yourself.

7. Reflect on what you have learned about yourself from this exercise and try to integrate this new understanding into your life.

THROUGH PROJECTION

You might be wondering how and why projection is necessary. The Freudian process lies at the center of the totality of our shadow, acting as a powerful defense mechanism that shields us from taking responsibility over any quality we dislike, yet practice (maybe unconsciously). It allows us to avoid coming face to face with our shortcomings. Of course, just as I had described the shadow self, it is not just negative traits that we project onto others, but sometimes positive ones as well, unconsciously ignoring them and refusing to admit that they are in us. This depends on how our egos are wired as we grow up.

Another point to know about projection is that it is not just limited to individuals but can be practiced by a social collective like friend groups, cults, political parties, towns, overall societies even. This generally has negative consequences as social issues such as racism, misogyny, homophobia, etc., can precipitate to the surface. Attacking another demographic group for qualities we might not want to acknowledge exist within us as a group is how projection can manifest itself on a large scale.

So how then can we use projection to uncover our shadow? Well, you have to understand that how you perceive others and the manner by which you judge them also reveals who you are and how you think. Your perception becomes a mirror into yourself and that is what you must use. With that, you should thus begin to cultivate an observant mind, analyzing the things you generally dislike (and like) in other people. Pen them down. Figure out what you project onto others and why you do so.

Even things like your favorite books, characters and movies can likewise reveal aspects of your shadow. Our interests in certain characters might reflect the secret of the kind of person we are. These are things you should study. Ask yourself why you prefer this character over the other. Why do you hate this movie in particular? What exactly is wrong with that genre that makes you cringe?

Your relationship with people also shows the nature of your projection. How do you react when your kid does something you don't like: is it with an exaggerated punishment? What about with your partner? Parents? Leave no stone unturned. The world is your mirror, so look into it and discover yourself.

ART THERAPY

Art should never be underestimated in its influence over our lives as it can allow you to access your shadow as you express yourself. Moreover, it's super easy and fun to practice, and gain an opportunity to develop a skill in the process. Art therapy has been used in the field of psychology over the years to study and restructure the mind of the individual.

What do you need to do to start? Well, all you have to do is pick up a blank piece of canvas and draw away. Let all those thoughts, both conscious and unconscious, be released as you paint. Let your shadow take the wheel and freely express whatever it is that comes to mind, regardless of how ridiculous or bizarre they might seem. They actually hold a secret to your shadow.

Always remember to be open-minded when you are doing this exercise.

WRITING A STORY

You could start working on a story where you explore the different suppressed parts of yourself, projecting the traits onto the various characters and analyzing yourself further from how they interact with each other. This will help illuminate the hidden aspects within you and help you achieve spiritual balance and wholeness.

PATIENCE IS KEY

Shadow work is not something you just finish in an hour or day. No, no, no. It is a lifelong journey. Repression will always take place as the days pass, newer projections will be formed and you might feel or feel utterly terrible after a while, but don't give up. All of it is part of the process. Breathe in and out because it's going to be alright.

Dream Analysis in a Nutshell

Dreams often contain archetypal elements that provide profound insights into the recesses of your subconscious. As you analyze recurring dream settings, characters, and symbols, and contemplate both their personal significance and their universal meanings, you'll unlock a deeper comprehension of the intricate symbolism through which your subconscious communicates with you. Whether these dreams manifest as vivid adventures or gentle whispers, each one carries a unique message! To unveil the recurring patterns in your dreams:

RECORD YOUR DREAMS

Consider keeping a dream journal within arm's reach of your bed. Dreams are fleeting, and capturing them as soon as you wake can wield significant insight. Upon waking, jot down the details of your dream in your journal: include the setting, characters, emotions, and any significant events. Over time, review your dream journal and look for common threads. Pay attention to the places where your dreams unfold. Is there a location that appears frequently, such as a childhood home, a school, or a specific city? The recurrence of a particular setting might suggest it holds significance in your life or symbolizes certain emotions or memories. Examine the characters in your dreams, whether they are people you know or complete strangers. Note the roles they play and the emotions they evoke. Are there individuals who consistently appear as mentors, adversaries, or allies? Reoccurring characters may represent different facets of your own personality or unresolved relationships. Recurring characters may embody different facets of your own personality or point to unresolved relationships.

EMBRACE SYMBOLISM

Dreams often speak in symbols. Pay attention to recurring symbols or objects. They might hold personal significance or represent aspects of your life. Here's how to decode the symbolism in your dreams:

Symbolic Objects or Events: Look for recurring objects, events, or actions in your dreams. These symbols might not be immediately apparent in your daily life, but they can carry profound meaning. For instance, a ladder could symbolize ambition or progress, while flying might signify freedom or liberation.

Personal Significance: Consider the personal significance of symbols. An object or symbol that frequently appears in your dreams might have a unique meaning for you, based on your life experiences and associations. For example, a rose might symbolize love and beauty to one person but signify thorns and challenges to another.

Collective Symbols: Some symbols have universal meanings that are recognized across cultures and throughout history. Carl Jung referred to these as "archetypal symbols." These symbols, like a circle representing wholeness or a serpent symbolizing transformation, tap into our shared human experiences.

EMOTIONAL CONTEXT

Pay attention to the emotions associated with symbols or events in your dreams. The emotional tone of a dream can offer insights into the message it carries. For example, encountering a snake may evoke fear in one dream but curiosity in another, leading to different interpretations.

Note Emotional Resonance: Understanding the emotional landscape of your dreams is a vital aspect of dream analysis. Emotions are the core language of the subconscious, and they offer significant clues to the meaning of your dreams. Here's how to explore the emotional context of your dreams:

Identify Dominant Emotions: As you review your dream journal, take note of the primary emotions you experience during your dreams. Are there recurring feelings such as fear, joy, anger, confusion, or curiosity? These emotions often serve as emotional guideposts in your dream analysis.

Emotional Changes: Pay attention to how your emotions evolve throughout the dream. Do you start with one emotion and transition to another? The sequence of emotional changes can provide insights into the narrative arc of the dream and your inner conflicts or desires.

Emotional Intensity: Consider the intensity of your emotions in the dream. Are they heightened or subdued? Intense emotions in a dream may signify unresolved issues or suppressed feelings in your waking life. Subdued emotions could indicate emotional distance or detachment from certain aspects of your reality.

Emotional Associations: Reflect on the events, characters, or symbols in your dreams that trigger specific emotions. Are there particular triggers that consistently evoke certain feelings? These triggers can be powerful indicators of what your subconscious is trying to communicate.

Emotional Relevance: Connect the emotions you experience in your dreams to your waking life. Are there parallel situations or unresolved emotional matters that align with the emotions in your dreams? Understanding how dream emotions relate to your real-life experiences can provide profound insights.

Emotions

Affection: A warm and tender feeling of fondness or love towards someone or something.

Amusement: A feeling of amusement or entertainment.

Anger: A strong feeling of displeasure or hostility.

Anxiety: A state of uneasiness and worry.

Anticipation: A hopeful or eager expectation of something positive.

Apathy: A lack of interest or emotional responsiveness.

Awe: A sense of wonder and amazement.

Boredom: A state of disinterest or lack of engagement.

Calm: A peaceful and tranquil state of mind.

Compassion: A deep sympathy and concern for others' suffering.

Confidence: A sense of self-assuredness and belief in one's abilities.

Confusion: A state of bewilderment or lack of clarity.

Contentment: A feeling of satisfaction and peace with one's current state.

Curiosity: A strong desire to explore or learn about something new.

Doubt: Uncertainty or skepticism about a decision or situation.

Empathy: The ability to understand and share the feelings of others.

Empowerment: A sense of strength and capability.

Enthusiasm: An intense passion or excitement for something.

Excitement: A heightened state of enthusiasm or eagerness.

Euphoria: An intense state of elation and happiness.

Fear: An emotional response to a perceived threat or danger.

Frustration: A feeling of annoyance or disappointment.

Grief: Intense sorrow, often in response to loss.

Gratitude: A feeling of thankfulness and appreciation.

Guilty: A feeling of remorse or responsibility for a wrongdoing.

Happiness: A state of well-being and contentedness.

Hope: A positive expectation for a desirable outcome.

Indifference: A lack of interest or concern.

Irritation: A feeling of annoyance or aggravation.

Jealousy: A combination of insecurity, fear of loss, and envy.

Joy: A deep sense of happiness or delight.

Loneliness: A sense of isolation and lack of social connection.

Love: A profound and intense affection or attachment to someone or something.

Lust: A strong desire or craving, often of a sexual nature.

Melancholy: A deep and lingering sadness.

Nervousness: A state of unease or restlessness.

Nostalgia: A longing for the past or sentimental feelings about it.

Panic: An overwhelming sense of fear and anxiety.

Pity: A feeling of sorrow and sympathy for someone's misfortune.

Pride: A sense of self-respect and satisfaction in one's achievements.

Regret: A sense of remorse or sorrow for past actions.

Relief: A feeling of comfort or alleviation of stress.

Resentment: A lingering feeling of anger or bitterness.

Sadness: A feeling of sorrow or unhappiness.

Satisfaction: A sense of fulfillment and contentment.

Serenity: A deep sense of inner peace and tranquility.

Shame: A painful emotion resulting from a sense of disgrace or humiliation.

Skepticism: A questioning and doubtful attitude.

Surprise: A sudden feeling of astonishment or shock.

Thankfulness: A feeling of gratitude and appreciation.

Tenderness: A gentle and affectionate emotion.

Wonder: A state of awe and fascination. sadness.

EMBRACE YOUR ARCHETYPE

THE 12 ARCHETYPES

Both Freud and Jung agreed that the mind was composed of a number of separate systems that influenced one another. According to Jung, the parts that composed our psyche were the ego, the personal unconscious and the collective unconscious. The ego represented all our thoughts and emotions that we were aware of. Our sense of identity is derived from the ego and through our memories, we also develop a sense of continuity. The unconscious part of the mind was where they had a disagreement. Freud only saw the unconscious as one single unit, whereas Jung further divided them into the personal unconscious and the collective unconscious. He notes that the personal unconscious was what Freud was occupied with, while the collective unconscious was the one Jung found more important in understanding human psychic life.

So, this personal unconscious that Freud favored was limited to a single individual. All the memories and emotions repressed in the past reside there. The information buried there laid out of the reach of the conscious mind unless they were somehow encountered in our dreams.

For Jung, however, he felt like the personal unconscious was simply a superficial layer; he believed that the one deserving of more attention in the understand of the psyche and treatment of neurotic disorders was the collective unconscious. This was a unique kind of unconscious that was shared by different individuals, unlike its personal counterpart. Jung also proposed it as a way to deny the philosopher John Locke's claim that we were born as blank slates. No, for Jung, we were anything but blank slates, as each of us possessed from birth the same unconscious layer. He argued that the reason why the different cultures around the world across time shared similar themes or had recurring similar characters was because of the collective unconscious that was shared by all.

Within this collective unconscious were archetypes. These universal symbols representing man's experiences and emotions were the bedrock for our personalities.

THE FOUR MAIN ARCHETYPES

You must have already heard about archetypes before coming here. Perhaps from your self-healing journey, in movies and books, wherever. What then are these things called archetypes? Carl Jung developed the system of archetypes as a tool for psychological analysis that were essentially model images of a person or role: a kind of ideal from which everyone else identified with. These archetypes resided in the collective unconscious and they reflected our basic human nature — the qualities universal to all of us. These archetypes are present in myths, legends and stories from all cultures around the world.

The most dominant archetypes are usually passed down from one generation to another, subtly shaping our personality traits and actions. These archetypes are necessary for attaining spiritual wholeness and self-realization. Understanding these archetypes can help you better uncover the repressed aspects of your mind from the depths of the unconscious. Your consciousness becomes expanded and elevated as your knowledge of your mind deepens, allowing for perfect integration.

Jung identified four major archetypes but also believed that there was no limit to the number that may exist. The existence of these archetypes cannot be observed directly but can be inferred by looking at religion, dreams, art and literature. Jung's four major archetypes are: the persona, the shadow, the anima/animus and the self.

1. The Persona

The persona, as I had explained earlier, was the mask we wore to cover our inner self and give ourselves a sense of identity. But these personas can easily be influenced by society and its structure. The persona is nothing more than an ideal or a wish the individual desires. It is who the person wants to be, not who they are. Therefore, complete association with one's persona can lead to further repression of their individuality. This is why it is also essential for the persona to undergo disintegration, in order to allow the person to grow after the chaos of the breakdown.

2. The Shadow Archetype

All the qualities of ourselves we don't wish to confront constitute this archetype. It is formed from our attempt to adapt to the norms of our culture, where all the repressed contents coalesce to form the shadow. They can manifest themselves in dreams or visions, so understanding them helps us approach our unconscious mind better.

3. The Animus/Anima Archetypes

Among the Jungian archetypes, the Animus and Anima are unique images built from the contents of the collective unconscious as well as from personal experience. The male image in the female's psyche was the Animus, while the feminine image in the male's psyche was the Anima. The animus and anima were not fixed identities, but rather fluid and evolving aspects of the psyche. They represented the masculine and feminine qualities that existed within every person, regardless of gender. As we grow up from childhood, we begin to develop a gender identity that is largely influenced by traditional cultural notions and norms. This influence causes us to repress the aspects that are unacceptable, and we pick one side. Men are discouraged from exploring their feminine sides, just as women are also instructed to discard their masculine aspects. This leaves us incomplete and undermines our overall spiritual development. It is vital that we explore and try to integrate these parts of our psyche in order to gain a deeper understanding of our personalities and relationships with others.

4. The Self

The Self is generally regarded as the totality of the consciousness and unconsciousness of the individual perfectly unified. It is the center of our personalities. The self is usually birthed from the process of individuation, where the various aspects of the psyche have been successfully integrated. The chaos resulting from the decomposition of the persona as well as the unearthing of the shadow allows for the unique opportunity to create a coherent and whole self. Jung represented the self as a circle, with a dot in the center that signified the ego that was at the helm of our consciousness.

THE 12 ARCHETYPICAL FIGURES

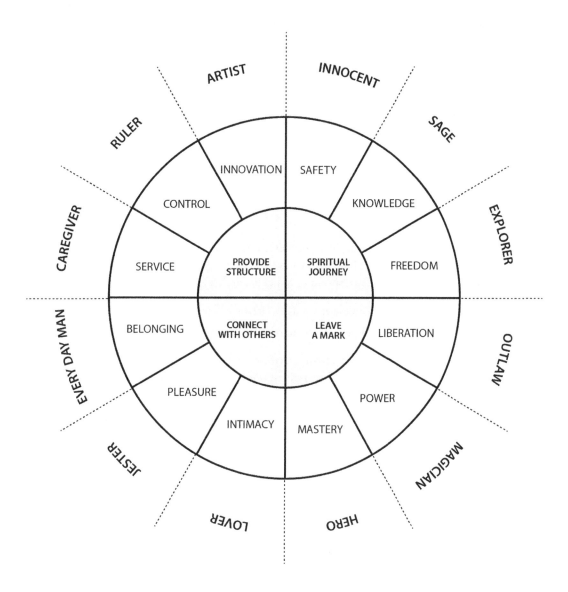

Beyond the four principal archetypical images, there have been over a hundred more archetypes defined over the years. These archetypes have been formed from the intermingling and interaction of the main archetypical figures. They can combine and overlap to form newer archetypes. The similarities between the dozens of archetypes described so far are pronounced, so they are mostly just reduced to 12 archetypes.

Most guides and materials on archetypical classifications usually work to foster identification with a single archetype. This leads one to lose sight of their individuality and whole selves. In actuality, all the 12 archetypical images already reside in our psyche. Of course, some are more pronounced than others, but that's all the more reason why work should be done in developing them.

These archetypes each have shadows of their own.

Identifying your archetype is often considered the first step towards shadow work. By identifying and acknowledging the shadow aspects of your archetype, you can begin to work on healing and integrating those parts of yourself that you may have been avoiding or rejecting.

For example, if your primary archetype is the Hero, your shadow may include a tendency towards arrogance or a need to always be in control. By recognizing these shadow aspects of your Hero archetype, you can begin to work on healing and integrating those parts of yourself that you may have been avoiding or rejecting.

Similarly, if your primary archetype is the Caregiver, your shadow may involve a tendency to be overly self-sacrificing or to struggle with setting boundaries. By acknowledging and working on these shadow aspects, you can develop a stronger sense of self-worth and the ability to care for others without sacrificing your own needs.

Ultimately, understanding your archetype and its shadow aspects can be a powerful tool in self-awareness and personal growth, allowing you to become more integrated and whole as a person.

You may be wondering how....

- Take an online quiz or assessment: There are many online quizzes and assessments available that can help you identify your archetype. These quizzes typically ask a series of questions about your personality, behavior, and preferences, and provide a result that corresponds to a specific archetype.

- Reflect on your life story: Another way to identify your archetype is to reflect on your life story and the themes that have emerged throughout your life. Think about the challenges you've faced, the goals you've pursued, and the relationships you've had, and look for patterns or themes that may correspond to a specific archetype.

- Consider your strengths and weaknesses: Each archetype is associated with certain strengths and weaknesses. Reflect on your own strengths and weaknesses and see if they align with any particular archetype.

Ultimately, the process of identifying your archetype may involve a combination of these approaches, as well as ongoing self-reflection and exploration. It's important to remember that archetypes are not fixed or static, and that you may identify with multiple archetypes or experience shifts in your dominant archetype over time.

In the following pages, you'll discover five journaling prompts designed to help you explore which archetype best aligns with your personal resonance.

Archetype Profiles

THE CAREGIVER

Appearance: The Caregiver archetype may appear as a warm and nurturing figure, often dressed in soft, comforting colors. They might exude a sense of gentleness and approachability.

Characteristics: This archetype embodies qualities of compassion, empathy, and selflessness. They may offer a listening ear and have a comforting presence.

Interactions and Relationships: The Caregiver often interacts with others in a nurturing and supportive way, offering comfort and care. They may have close, empathetic relationships with those they care for.

Emotions and Energies: This archetype radiates emotions of compassion, tenderness, and unconditional love. Their energy is calming and soothing, providing a sense of safety.

Power and Influence: The Caregiver's power lies in their ability to heal and support others. They have influence through their capacity to provide emotional and physical care.

Themes and Symbols: Common themes include caregiving, protection, and selflessness. Symbols may include a motherly figure, a gentle touch, or the image of a caregiver tending to others.

Intuition and Gut Feelings: You might feel a deep sense of warmth and comfort when the Caregiver appears, along with a desire for emotional connection and support.

THE REBEL

Appearance: Rebels often appear as individuals who defy societal norms. They may be dressed in unconventional clothing, sporting tattoos, or unique hairstyles, reflecting their non-conformist attitude.

Characteristics: The Rebel archetype is characterized by a strong desire for change and social justice. They challenge authority and may have a fiery and determined demeanor.

Interactions and Relationships: Rebels often engage in challenging conversations and interactions, pushing against established norms. They may form connections with fellow activists and free thinkers.

Emotions and Energies: This archetype embodies emotions of defiance, rebellion, and a drive for change. Their energy is fiery and passionate, sparking a sense of urgency.

Power and Influence: Rebels have the power to inspire social change and challenge the status quo. They influence through their courage to question authority.

Themes and Symbols: Themes include rebellion, social justice, and breaking free from constraints. Symbols might include protest signs, revolutionary imagery, or icons of defiance.

Intuition and Gut Feelings: You may sense a surge of determination and a desire to challenge the norm when the Rebel appears.

THE HERO

Appearance: Heroes often have a strong, confident presence. They may be dressed in attire that signifies their courage, like a knight in shining armor or a superhero in a bold costume.

Characteristics: The Hero embodies qualities of bravery, determination, and a sense of duty. They're driven to overcome challenges and protect others.

Interactions and Relationships: Heroes often form alliances and mentorships, guiding and protecting others. They may engage in heroic acts to save or uplift those in need.

Emotions and Energies: This archetype carries emotions of bravery, determination, and a deep sense of duty. Their energy is dynamic and courageous, inspiring action.

Power and Influence: Heroes have the power to lead and inspire others to face challenges. They influence through their unwavering commitment to their mission.

Themes and Symbols: Themes include heroism, bravery, and the call to adventure. Symbols might include swords, capes, or depictions of heroic deeds.

Intuition and Gut Feelings: When the Hero emerges, you may feel a surge of motivation and a readiness to take on challenges.

THE EXPLORER

Appearance: Explorers may appear in attire suitable for adventure, like hiking gear or explorer's clothing. They radiate a sense of curiosity and enthusiasm.

Characteristics: This archetype thrives on seeking new experiences, is open to change, and embodies a sense of adventure and a love for discovery.

Interactions and Relationships: Explorers seek companions who share their sense of adventure. They may form connections with fellow travelers and curious minds.

Emotions and Energies: This archetype embodies emotions of curiosity, wanderlust, and a thirst for new experiences. Their energy is adventurous and open-minded.

Power and Influence: Explorers have the power to broaden perspectives and discover the unknown. They influence through their willingness to embrace change.

Themes and Symbols: Themes include exploration, discovery, and the thrill of the journey. Symbols might include maps, compasses, or depictions of uncharted territories.

Intuition and Gut Feelings: When the Explorer appears, you may feel a pull toward new experiences and a sense of wonder about the world.

THE LOVER

Appearance: Lovers often appear with an aura of sensuality and romanticism. They might be dressed elegantly or in clothing that emphasizes their allure.

Characteristics: The Lover archetype values intimacy, connection, and emotional depth. They may exude warmth, passion, and a deep appreciation for beauty.

Interactions and Relationships: Lovers engage in deep and passionate relationships, valuing emotional connections. They may form bonds with those who share their sense of romance and sensuality.

Emotions and Energies: This archetype embodies emotions of love, sensuality, and a profound connection to others. Their energy is affectionate and alluring.

Power and Influence: Lovers have the power to ignite love and passion in themselves and others. They influence through their ability to create deep emotional bonds.

Themes and Symbols: Themes include romance, intimacy, and the pursuit of beauty. Symbols might include hearts, roses, or depictions of tender moments.

Intuition and Gut Feelings: When the Lover appears, you may sense a longing for deep emotional connections and a heightened appreciation for beauty.

THE SAGE

Appearance: Sages typically have a wise and contemplative demeanor. They may appear in scholarly attire or robes, with an air of intellectualism.

Characteristics: The Sage archetype represents wisdom, knowledge, and introspection. They often offer guidance and seek to unravel life's mysteries.

Interactions and Relationships: Sages often engage in mentorship and share wisdom with others. They may form connections with those who seek knowledge and guidance.

Emotions and Energies: This archetype embodies emotions of wisdom, curiosity, and a desire for understanding. Their energy is contemplative and insightful.

Power and Influence: Sages have the power to offer guidance and expand knowledge. They influence through their ability to provide valuable insights.

Themes and Symbols: Themes include wisdom, knowledge, and the pursuit of truth. Symbols might include books, scrolls, or depictions of intellectual exploration.

Intuition and Gut Feelings: When the Sage appears, you may sense a thirst for knowledge and a desire to seek wisdom.

THE JESTER

Appearance: Jesters have a playful and whimsical appearance. They might wear colorful, clown-like attire or clothing that reflects their jovial nature.

Characteristics: The Jester archetype embodies humor, spontaneity, and a knack for lightening the mood. They often bring joy and laughter to others.

Interactions and Relationships: Jesters bring humor and playfulness to interactions, often making others laugh. They may form connections with those who appreciate wit and spontaneity.

Emotions and Energies: This archetype embodies emotions of humor, spontaneity, and a love for playfulness. Their energy is lively and entertaining.

Power and Influence: Jesters have the power to lighten the mood and bring joy to others. They influence through their ability to create laughter and fun.

Themes and Symbols: Themes include humor, spontaneity, and the joy of the present moment. Symbols might include masks, jesters' hats, or depictions of playful antics.

Intuition and Gut Feelings: When the Jester appears, you may feel a sense of levity and a desire to embrace the lighter side of life.

THE CREATOR

Appearance: Creators may appear as individuals immersed in creative pursuits. They could be seen with art supplies or tools, reflecting their creative spirit.

Characteristics: The Creator archetype values innovation, artistic expression, and the act of bringing something new into the world.

Interactions and Relationships: Creators often collaborate with others on artistic or innovative projects. They may form connections with those who share their creative spirit.

Emotions and Energies: This archetype embodies emotions of creativity, innovation, and a drive to bring ideas to life. Their energy is imaginative and inventive.

Power and Influence: Creators have the power to inspire and bring forth new creations. They influence through their ability to manifest ideas into reality.

Themes and Symbols: Themes include creativity, innovation, and the act of bringing something new into the world. Symbols might include paintbrushes, canvases, or depictions of creative processes.

Intuition and Gut Feelings: When the Creator appears, you may feel a surge of inspiration and a desire to express your creativity.

THE EVERYMAN

Appearance: Everyman/Woman archetypes have a relatable and down-to-earth appearance. They may wear everyday clothing that reflects their simplicity.

Characteristics: This archetype resonates with the experiences and struggles of ordinary people. They find beauty in the familiar and prioritize humility and relatability.

Interactions and Relationships: Everyman/Woman archetypes engage in relatable and down-to-earth interactions. They form connections with those who value simplicity and authenticity.

Emotions and Energies: This archetype embodies emotions of humility, relatability, and an appreciation for the everyday. Their energy is grounded and unassuming.

Power and Influence: Everyman/Woman archetypes have the power to connect with people on a relatable level. They influence through their authenticity and relatability.

Themes and Symbols: Themes include relatability, humility, and the beauty in the familiar. Symbols might include everyday objects, simple clothing, or depictions of everyday life.

Intuition and Gut Feelings: When the Everyman/Woman appears, you may feel a sense of comfort and a connection to the simple joys of life.

THE RULER

Appearance: Rulers often appear in attire that signifies authority and leadership. They may carry symbols of power, like a crown or a scepter.

Characteristics: The Ruler archetype embodies leadership, responsibility, and a desire to create order and stability.

Interactions and Relationships: Rulers often engage in leadership roles and authoritative interactions. They may form connections with those who seek stability and structure.

Emotions and Energies: This archetype embodies emotions of authority, responsibility, and a desire to create order. Their energy is commanding and structured.

Power and Influence: Rulers have the power to lead and create structured environments. They influence through their ability to establish and maintain order.

Themes and Symbols: Themes include leadership, responsibility, and the pursuit of stability. Symbols might include crowns, scepters, or depictions of structured governance.

Intuition and Gut Feelings: When the Ruler appears, you may sense a desire for structure and a readiness to take charge.

THE INNOCENT

Appearance: Innocents have a pure and trusting appearance. They may wear simple, childlike clothing or attire that reflects their optimism.

Characteristics: The Innocent archetype values simplicity, purity, and the belief in the innate goodness of people and the world.

Interactions and Relationships: Innocents engage in interactions with a sense of purity and trust. They may form connections with those who appreciate innocence and simplicity.

Emotions and Energies: This archetype embodies emotions of purity, trust, and a belief in the innate goodness of people and the world. Their energy is gentle and optimistic.

Power and Influence: Innocents have the power to inspire trust and bring out the goodness in others. They influence through their ability to foster innocence and hope.

Themes and Symbols: Themes include innocence, purity, and the belief in goodness. Symbols might include white doves, children's toys, or depictions of idyllic settings.

Intuition and Gut Feelings: When the Innocent appears, you may feel a sense of trust and a belief in the goodness of the world.

THE MAGICIAN

Appearance: Magicians have an enigmatic and mystical appearance. They may be seen with symbolic items like a wand or a book of spells.

Characteristics: The Magician archetype embodies transformation, intuition, and a belief in the hidden potentials and mysteries of life.

Interactions and Relationships: Magicians engage in interactions that reflect their mystical and transformative nature. They may form connections with those who seek inner wisdom.

Emotions and Energies: This archetype embodies emotions of mystery, transformation, and a belief in hidden potentials. Their energy is enigmatic and inspiring.

Power and Influence: Magicians have the power to facilitate transformation and unlock hidden potentials. They influence through their ability to tap into the mystical and mysterious.

Themes and Symbols: Themes include transformation, mysticism, and the pursuit of hidden knowledge. Symbols might include magic wands, ancient texts, or depictions of mystical rituals.

Intuition and Gut Feelings: When the Magician appears, you may sense a desire for inner transformation and a fascination with the mysteries of life.

What motivates me in life?

Think about your values, passions, and goals. Do they reflect a desire for adventure and exploration (the Explorer archetype)? Or do you value stability and structure (the Ruler archetype)? Write about what drives you and why.

What are my strengths and weaknesses?

Each archetype has its strengths and weaknesses. For example, the Hero archetype is courageous and selfless, but can also be arrogant and reckless. The Sage archetype is wise and analytical, but can also be detached and aloof. Think about your own strengths and weaknesses and consider which archetype they align with.

Who are my role models or heroes?

The people we look up to can reveal a lot about our own archetypal preferences. Do you admire rebels and rule-breakers (the Outlaw archetype)? Or do you idolize leaders and visionaries (the Creator archetype)? Write about the people you admire and why.

What are my recurring dreams or fantasies?

Dreams and fantasies can also provide clues about our archetypal tendencies. Do you dream about exploring new worlds and pushing boundaries (the Explorer archetype)? Or do you fantasize about creating new things and leaving a lasting legacy (the Creator archetype)? Reflect on your recurring dreams or fantasies and see if they align with any of the archetypes.

What challenges have I faced in life, and how have I overcome them?

Each archetype faces its own set of challenges. For example, the Innocent archetype may struggle with naivete and disillusionment, while the Magician archetype may face skepticism and doubt. Think about the challenges you've faced in your life and how you've overcome them. Consider which archetypes resonate with your experiences and approach to problem-solving.

THE RULER ARCHETYPE

ALSO KNOWN AS
The Leader, The Boss, The King/Queen

TALENT
Authority, responsibility, and the ability to manage
and lead others

CORE DESIRE
To create a prosperous and harmonious society, and
exercise control and power over others.

MAIN GOAL
To create a prosperous and harmonious society

MOTTO
Power isn't everything, it's the only thing

FATAL FLAW
Control freak

ADDICTION
Power

The ruler archetype represents leadership, power, and the desire to create order and stability. It is often associated with the desire to be in control and make decisions for others, thus providing structure to the lives of everyone around them. The ruler seeks to create a sense of order and structure in the world.

The Ruler archetype has the power to achieve any goal set before them. In fact, they enjoy it. In putting these goals to action, they are also able to draw people to join their cause. Their confidence, logical thinking and vision inspires those around them to support them.

This archetype is very important in structure creation and order preservation in the environment around them, and a failure to integrate this archetype into your Self leads one to descend into chaos.

THE SHADOW RULER ARCHETYPE

The shadow of the ruler is the desire for absolute power and control that can come with a desire for leadership. This can lead to a lack of empathy or a disregard for the well-being of others. A shadow projection may also make you a strict authoritarian, both at work and at home. This is a weakness in character that can be overcome by releasing repressed anger and adopting the qualities of the lover archetype.

Because the tyrannical ruler wants complete control, people that are possessed by this archetype find it difficult to delegate. In such cases, the shadow energies will appear in the form of feeling overwhelmed. This is an indication for you to stop putting too many demands on yourself and learn to trust others.

When the Ruler archetype is underdeveloped, people will not admit they cannot do something in case it undermines their authority. This also reflects deep-rooted feelings that you are not good enough.

The Hero archetype is the ideal counterpart for the Ruler in developing your coherent Self. When you detect traits of the shadow king within yourself, employ the warrior in you.

EMBRACE YOUR SENSE OF RESPONSIBILITY AND AUTHORITY

Here are some more practical examples of exercises that can help the Ruler archetype cultivate a sense of responsibility and leadership:

1. Take on a leadership role: Seek out opportunities to take on a leadership role in your workplace, community or personal life. This could involve leading a team or project, organizing an event or initiative or mentoring others.

2. Set goals and priorities: Develop a clear vision for what you want to achieve and set specific goals and priorities to help you achieve it. Use tools like a vision board, goal-setting software or a planner to help you stay organized and focused.

3. Develop your decision-making skills: Practice making tough decisions and taking decisive action. Use techniques like pro-con lists or decision trees to help you weigh the pros and cons of different options and make informed choices.

4. Build your communication skills: Cultivate clear and effective communication skills that will help you articulate your vision, motivate others and resolve conflicts. Practice active listening, public speaking and negotiation skills.

5. Seek out mentorship and coaching: Connect with experienced leaders in your field or industry who can provide guidance and support as you develop your leadership skills. Consider hiring a coach or joining a mastermind group to help you stay accountable and motivated.

Remember, the key to developing the Ruler archetype is to embrace your sense of responsibility and authority, while also being compassionate and empathetic towards others. With practice, you can cultivate the skills and qualities you need to become a confident and effective leader in all aspects of your life.

AFFIRMATIONS FOR THE RULER ARCHETYPE

- I am confident in my leadership abilities.

- I trust in my decisions and actions.

- I am capable of creating a positive impact on the world.

- I have the power to make a difference.

- I am respected and valued by those around me.

- I am deserving of success and prosperity.

- I embrace my authority and use it for the greater good.

- I am a visionary and inspire others to follow my lead.

- I lead with integrity and honor.

- I am a natural born leader and guide.

PROMPTS FOR THE RULER ARCHETYPE

What is your vision for your ideal life, and how can you take steps to make it a reality?

How can you establish healthy boundaries in your personal and professional relationships?

How can you use your power and influence to positively impact your community or organization?

What values are most important to you, and how can you ensure that your actions align with those values?

What actions can you take to cultivate a sense of stability and security in your life?

How can you inspire and motivate others to take action towards a common goal?

What leadership qualities do you possess, and how can you continue to develop and refine them?

How can you balance the needs of the collective with the needs of the individual?

What challenges do you face in your leadership role, and how can you overcome them?

How can you delegate responsibilities effectively to others while still maintaining a sense of control?

How can you use your resources and assets to create positive change in the world?

What steps can you take to create a supportive and nurturing environment for those around you?

How can you foster a sense of trust and loyalty among those who work with you?

What measures can you put in place to ensure accountability and transparency in your leadership?

How can you use your voice and platform to advocate for important causes or issues?

What legacy do you want to leave behind, and how can you work towards that legacy?

How can you cultivate a sense of respect and admiration from those who look up to you?

What risks are worth taking in order to achieve your goals?

How can you handle power and authority responsibly and ethically?

How can you continue to learn and grow as a leader and as a person?

What is one decision or responsibility that you've had to make as a leader or authority figure, and how did you balance your own needs with the needs of others?

THE CREATOR ARCHETYPE

ALSO KNOWN AS
The Artist, The Inventor, The Innovator

TALENT
Imagination, originality, and the ability to create
something new and valuable

CORE DESIRE
To bring something new into the world and leave a
lasting legacy

MAIN GOAL
To bring something new and valuable into the world

MOTTO
If you can imagine it, it can be done

FATAL FLAW
Perfectionism

ADDICTION
Creativity

The Creator, also known as the artist, archetype represents creativity, imagination and the desire to bring new things into the world. It is often associated with the desire to express oneself through art or other forms of creation. The Creator seeks to express their unique vision and bring something new into the world. This potent imagination inspires you with a strong desire to achieve your goals and bring your vision to reality.

While both the Ruler and the Creator share a passion for providing structure to their environment, they are inherently different in their mindset. This vision furnished by the Creator finally gets adopted by the ruler. The Creator is content with the process of creation and derives pleasure from the things they have successfully made. Concerns about the absolute control of the vision is usually a quality of the Ruler archetype.

Along with this ardor for imagination and creation of ideas is the drive to learn, relearn and adapt according to the changes around them. This is especially useful given the advance in technology today.

All in all, the Creator wishes to continuously improve themselves and this is a trait that enables one to become their best selves.

THE SHADOW CREATOR ARCHETYPE

The shadow of the creator is the tendency to be overly critical of one's own work or to become obsessed with perfection. Negative traits of the Creator archetype can often cause you to lose sight of what you have achieved. This can lead to a lack of productivity or a fear of failure.

When you focus on perfection, you struggle to accept things for how they are. The inability to be content with what you have and move on is obviously a detriment to self-development. Unless you explore other aspects of life, you cannot develop your personality and ultimately become stale.

Moreover, whilst you pursue the ultimate creation, you lack stability and comfort. Artist personalities tend to live in their heads and are often not in control of their emotions. Emotional discharges can create beautiful art, but typically create chaos in your life.

As a consequence, this can affect and shatter your connection with your relationships. By excluding other people, you develop the same negative traits as the Ruler is unable to delegate.

Cultivate a sense of imagination and self-expression

Here are some practical exercises that can help the Creator archetype cultivate their sense of imagination and self-expression:

1. Start a creative project: Whether it's painting, writing or crafting, start a project that allows you to express your creativity. Set aside time each day or week to work on your project and see it through to completion.

2. Take a class or workshop: Sign up for a class or workshop in a creative field that interests you. This could be anything from a painting class to a writing workshop to a cooking course. Learning new techniques and skills can help you expand your creative abilities.

3. Explore new mediums: Try working in a medium or art form that you've never tried before. Experiment with new tools and techniques to see what sparks your imagination and creativity.

4. Collaborate with others: Connect with other creatives and collaborate on a project together. This could be a group art show, a co-writing project or a music collaboration. Working with others can help you generate new ideas and approaches to your craft.

5. Take inspiration from your surroundings: Look to your surroundings for inspiration. Take a walk-in nature, explore your city or visit a museum or art exhibit. Take note of what catches your eye and use it as inspiration for your creative projects.

Embrace your unique perspective and creative vision, and don't be afraid to experiment and take risks. With practice, you can develop your skills and find fulfillment in expressing yourself creatively.

AFFIRMATIONS FOR THE CREATOR ARCHETYPE

*   I am a visionary, with a unique and creative perspective on the world.

*   I am an artist, bringing beauty and meaning into the world through my work.

*   I am a master of my craft, constantly honing my skills and pushing the boundaries of what is possible.

*   I am a source of inspiration, inspiring others to create and innovate in their own lives.

*   I am a channel for the divine, allowing my creativity to flow through me and into the world.

*   I am open to new ideas and experiences, constantly seeking out inspiration and new sources of creativity.

*   I am confident in my own abilities and talents, and I trust in my intuition to guide me.

- I am willing to take risks and try new things, even if they are outside of my comfort zone.

- I am committed to bringing my creative visions to life, no matter what obstacles may arise.

- I am a Creator, and I embrace my role in shaping the world with my unique gifts and talents.

PROMPTS FOR THE CREATOR ARCHETYPE

What inspires you to create, and how do you channel this inspiration into your work?

What do you hope to achieve through your creations, and how do you measure success?

How do you balance your desire for perfection with the need to take risks and experiment?

How do you deal with creative blocks or periods of low inspiration, and what strategies do you use to overcome them?

How do you find your unique voice and style, and what steps do you take to develop and refine it?

What do you consider your greatest masterpiece, and what makes it special to you?

How do you collaborate with others, and what strategies do you use to balance your own vision with the needs and desires of your collaborators?

How do you stay connected to your audience and their needs and desires, and how does this impact your creative process?

How do you balance your creative work with the practical aspects of running a business or making a living?

How do you deal with criticism or rejection, and what strategies do you use to stay motivated and continue creating?

What is your definition of creativity and innovation?

How do you cultivate a sense of curiosity and imagination in your life?

What role does art, music, or other creative pursuits play in your life?

Describe a moment when you felt truly inspired.

What is your approach to problem-solving and finding solutions?

How do you stay motivated and focused on your creative projects?

How do you handle criticism or setbacks in your creative work?

What is your process for generating new ideas?

How do you stay true to your artistic vision while still meeting practical constraints?

How do you balance the need for structure and planning with the need for spontaneity and experimentation?

What is one project or idea that you've been passionate about but haven't yet pursued, and what steps can you take to make it a reality?

THE INNOCENT ARCHETYPE

ALSO KNOWN AS
The Utopian, The Dreamer, The Idealist

TALENT
Optimism, faith, and simplicity

CORE DESIRE
To find happiness and a sense of paradise

MAIN GOAL
To be happy and find paradise

MOTTO
Free to be you and me

FATAL FLAW
Naivety

ADDICTION
Safety

The Innocent archetype, or the Child, represents purity, goodness and simplicity. It is often associated with childhood and the desire to experience life in a positive and joyful way. The Innocent seeks to maintain a sense of goodness and purity in the world, and often has a childlike sense of wonder and curiosity about the world around them. This air of innocence about them is highly contagious and can often inspire in the people around them a sense of tranquility and optimism.

Because of the purity of thought in this archetype, the Innocent finds it very easy to forgive those that had hurt them in the past, and as a result, grow beyond the darkness of hate. It is thus very important to integrate this archetype into your Self.

THE SHADOW INNOCENT ARCHETYPE

The shadow of the innocent is the naivety and gullibility that can come with a lack of life experience. This can lead to being taken advantage of or being too trusting of others.

Because the survival of the Innocent is dependent on others, people with a dominant child archetype are more inclined to follow and obey. This can make them lack responsibility and ignore reality.

It is often the case that people living a sheltered life are strongly influenced by the Innocent archetype. They have subsequently grown into an adult-child and harbor childish personality traits.

You might also be precocious and difficult to reason with. Moreover, you shy away from challenges and ignore anything that goes wrong. In doing so, you invite more problems into your life moving forward.

However, every problem or situation you encounter in life is an opportunity to learn something about yourself. The shadow side of the Innocent archetype acts as a catalyst for growth.

To overcome the shadow nature of the Innocent archetype, individuals have to call upon the hero or explorer archetypes, both of which are subclasses of the hero archetype.

CULTIVATE A SENSE OF WONDER AND OPTIMISM

Here are some practical exercises that can help the Innocent archetype cultivate their sense of optimism and wonder:

1. Practice gratitude: Take time each day to reflect on the things in your life that you're grateful for. This could be as simple as a warm cup of tea or a kind word from a friend. Focusing on the positive aspects of your life can help you cultivate a sense of optimism and joy.

2. Connect with nature: Spend time in nature and take in the beauty of the world around you. Go for a hike, take a walk in the park or simply sit outside and observe the natural world. This can help you cultivate a sense of wonder and appreciation for the world around you.

3. Embrace playfulness: Allow yourself to be playful and childlike. Engage in activities that bring you joy and make you feel care-free, such as playing a game or trying a new hobby.

4. Engage in volunteer work: Find a cause or organization that you feel passionate about and volunteer your time and energy. Giving back can help you cultivate a sense of purpose and fulfillment.

5. Seek out new experiences: Try new things. This could be as simple as trying a new restaurant or taking a trip to a new city. Opening yourself up to new experiences can help you cultivate a sense of curiosity and excitement about the world.

Embrace the joy of discovery and focus on the positive aspects of life. With practice, you can develop a childlike sense of wonder and appreciation for the world around you.

AFFIRMATIONS FOR THE INNOCENT ARCHETYPE

- I trust in the goodness of others.

- I am capable of achieving my dreams and desires.

- I am pure and true to myself.

- I have an open and curious mind.

- I see the world with wonder and awe.

- I believe in hope and optimism.

- I am innocent, but not naive.

- I am protected and safe in the world.

- I am deserving of love and happiness.

- I radiate light and positivity wherever I go.

PROMPTS FOR THE INNOCENT ARCHETYPE

What brings you the most joy and happiness in life, and how can you cultivate more of those experiences?

What are some of your most cherished childhood memories, and how can you tap into the feelings they evoke?

How can you maintain a sense of optimism and positivity in the face of challenges or setbacks?

What are some ways you can approach life with a sense of wonder and curiosity?

What beliefs or values do you hold that help you navigate the world with a sense of trust and innocence?

How can you maintain a sense of playfulness and lightness in your daily life?

What small, simple pleasures can you enjoy on a regular basis to bring a sense of joy and innocence to your day?

How can you cultivate a sense of purity and naivete without becoming naive or gullible?

What kind of environment or surroundings help you feel safe and secure?

How can you approach new experiences with a sense of openness and excitement, rather than fear or skepticism?

What can you do to maintain a sense of trust in the world and in others, even when things don't go as planned?

How can you use your innocence and optimism to inspire and uplift others?

What are some of the ways you can embrace your vulnerability and openness, without becoming too sensitive or overly trusting?

How can you stay true to your authentic self, even in the face of societal pressure or expectation?

What kind of self-care practices can help you maintain a sense of innocence and purity in your own life?

How can you use your sense of wonder and curiosity to approach life's challenges with a creative and innovative mindset?

What kind of relationships and connections help you feel most safe and secure, and how can you cultivate those in your life?

What can you do to approach life's challenges with a sense of faith and trust, rather than fear or anxiety?

How can you maintain a sense of idealism and hope, even in the face of disappointment or adversity?

What are some of the ways you can use your innocence and pure heart to make a positive impact on the world around you?

What is one thing you wish you could un-learn or forget in order to regain a sense of childlike wonder and trust in the world?

THE CAREGIVER ARCHETYPE

ALSO KNOWN AS
The Nurturer, The Protector, The Helper

TALENT
Compassion, empathy, and the ability to care for
others

CORE DESIRE
To help and support others, and create a safe and
secure environment for them

MAIN GOAL
To protect and care for others

MOTTO
Love your neighbor as yourself

FATAL FLAW
Martyrdom

ADDICTION
Helping others

The Caregiver is one of the most important archetypes one can develop. The Caregiver archetype, or the mother archetype, represents nurturing, compassion, and the desire to care for others. It is often associated with the desire to help others and create a sense of safety and security. The Caregiver seeks to create a sense of comfort and well-being for those around them, and this endears you in their eyes.

Just like a mother would, the Caregiver is deeply loving and generally puts the needs of others before their own. They are protective of the ones they love and are primarily concerned with nurturing their "child". Of course, they are also able to say no to their offspring, since they know what is best for them, and are also flexible enough to provide a comfortable space that lets them grow.

THE SHADOW CAREGIVER ARCHETYPE

The shadow of the caregiver is the tendency to neglect one's own needs in order to care for others. This can lead to burnout or a lack of self-care. By giving yourself excessively to others, you lose your sense of self and find it difficult to set boundaries. Thus, they neglect to meet their basic physical or emotional needs. If the caregiver in you is unable to set boundaries, the shadow will appear as feelings of bitterness and resentment. You may even guilt-trip people so they recognize your sacrifices. Ultimately, you want to be recognized for your good deeds to feed your emotional body.

If the caregiver in you is unable to set boundaries, the shadow will appear as feelings of bitterness and resentment. You may even guilt-trip people so they recognize your sacrifices. Ultimately, you want to be recognized for your good deeds to feed your emotional body.

Shadow energies of the Caregiver archetype also surface as feelings of inadequacy. This can quickly lead to anger and frustration which ultimately dissolves all positive aspects of the Caregiver's loving and compassionate nature.

Negative aspects of the Caregiver can arise due to a mother complex, where, because of lack of emotional support from your mother, you develop strong feelings of inadequacy. As an adult, you can often feel overwhelmed with situations you think are beyond your realm of capability. This makes you feel incompetent and unworthy – again, feelings that were instilled in childhood because your achievements or your presence was not recognized.

Caregivers can also develop a slave mentality which leaves you feeling exhausted. When you are not in a position to do something for somebody else – when you have to say no – you feel guilty and ashamed.

The negative mother is the shadow type of the Caregiver archetype. It represents the desire for control and manipulation, and it can manifest in negative behaviors such as emotional abuse and neglect. The negative mother represents the part of us that wants to control and manipulate others, and it is often associated with feelings of guilt and shame.

CULTIVATE THEIR SENSE OF COMPASSION AND EMPATHY

Here are some practical exercises that can help the Caregiver archetype cultivate their sense of compassion and empathy:

1. Practice active listening: Take the time to truly listen to the people in your life. This means giving them your full attention and being present in the moment. Ask questions, show empathy and offer support where you can.

2. Volunteer your time: Find a local charity or organization that you feel passionate about and volunteer your time and energy. This could involve working with children, the elderly or those in need of medical or emotional support.

3. Take care of yourself: In order to be an effective caregiver, it's important to take care of yourself first. Make sure you're getting enough rest, exercise and nourishing food; remember to always seek out support when you need it.

4. Practice forgiveness: Let go of grudges and practice forgiveness towards those who have wronged you. This can help you cultivate a sense of compassion and empathy towards others.

5. Nurture your relationships: Cultivate strong, supportive relationships with the people in your life. Take the time to show appreciation for their kindness and support and be there for them when they need you.

By practicing active listening, volunteering your time, and taking care of yourself, you can develop the skills and qualities you need to be an effective caregiver in all aspects of your life.

AFFIRMATIONS FOR THE CAREGIVER ARCHETYPE

- I am compassionate and empathetic towards others.

- I have a natural ability to nurture and care for those in need.

- I am strong and resilient in the face of adversity.

- I am able to give and receive love freely.

- I make a positive impact on the lives of others.

- I am deserving of self-care and rest.

- I am patient and understanding with myself and others.

- I have the ability to heal and bring comfort to others.

- I am a source of strength and support for those around me.

- I am a natural caretaker and nurturer.

PROMPTS FOR THE CAREGIVER ARCHETYPE

Who are the people in your life that you care for the most, and how can you prioritize their needs while also taking care of your own?

What are some ways you can practice self-compassion and self-care to avoid burnout and maintain your own well-being as a caregiver?

How can you approach caring for others with a sense of empathy and understanding, even when it is challenging or draining?

What kind of boundaries can you set to ensure that you are not taking on more than you can handle as a caregiver?

How can you use your nurturing and compassionate nature to support and uplift those around you?

What kind of support systems can you rely on when you need a break or assistance in your caregiving role?

What are some ways you can approach caregiving with a sense of creativity and innovation, to find new solutions and approaches to challenges?

How can you maintain a sense of balance and harmony in your relationships with those you care for, while also setting boundaries and asserting your own needs?

What kind of resources and tools can you access to help you be a more effective caregiver?

How can you use your caregiving role to make a positive impact on your community or society as a whole?

What kind of self-reflection and self-awareness practices can help you avoid falling into patterns of co-dependency or over-caregiving?

How can you approach caregiving with a sense of gratitude and appreciation, rather than feeling burdened or resentful?

What are some ways you can use your caregiving role to learn and grow as a person, both personally and professionally?

How can you approach difficult conversations or conflicts with those you care for with a sense of compassion and understanding?

What kind of self-talk and inner dialogue can help you maintain a positive and uplifting mindset as a caregiver?

How can you use your natural inclination towards nurturing and caretaking to build and strengthen your relationships with others?

What kind of education or training can you pursue to enhance your skills as a caregiver?

How can you approach your caregiving role with a sense of patience and persistence, even when progress is slow or challenging?

What are some ways you can build and maintain a support system of other caregivers to share resources, experiences, and support?

How can you use your caregiving role to make a positive impact on the world around you, and inspire others to also prioritize care and compassion in their own lives?

What is one act of kindness or selflessness that you've done for someone else, and how did it make you feel?

HOW TO MEET YOUR TRUE SELF

THE EVERYMAN ARCHETYPE

ALSO KNOWN AS
The Good Neighbor, The Homemaker, The Person
Next Door

TALENT

Reliability, loyalty, and a sense of belonging

CORE DESIRE
To connect with others and find acceptance in the
community

MAIN GOAL
To belong and feel valued

MOTTO
All men and women are created equal

FATAL FLAW
Losing one's own identity

ADDICTION
Familiarity

Integral to the Everyman archetype is the desire to fit in to a community. They have the ability to easily connect and forge strong bonds with others, thanks to their friendly personality.

This regular guy/girl archetype (as it can also be called) represents relatability, or commonality,. It is often associated with the desire to be seen as "normal" or "average". The regular guy/girl seeks to be accepted by their peers and fit in with societal norms, and they are very likeable in their social circle. This allows them to relate well with others and achieve shared goals easily without any desire for power, since they are content with the simple task of just carrying out their job in the team.

It is easy to see that the Everyman shares certain traits with the Innocent, especially with their yearning for a sense of safety that's only achieved by belonging to a community. Of course, this can naturally lead to a vulnerability.

THE SHADOW EVERYMAN ARCHETYPE

The gravest fear in the Everyman archetype is to feel left out. Being ignored is devastating and this leads them to become dependent on others. This can give you an aura of weakness or helplessness, which might go on to hinder further self-development. In some people, they might deliberately avoid learning, so that others can do it for them. As a result, when the Orphan archetype is dominant, you may emotionally manipulate people to give them a guilt trip.

The shadow of the regular guy/girl is the conformity and lack of individuality that can come with a desire to fit in. This can lead to a lack of creativity or a fear of standing out from the crowd.

An underdeveloped Everyman archetype will also prompt you to conform with societal norms and the demands of people you want to like you. This will often lead to you saying yes to things you don't really want to do.

Moreover, the more you conform to what other people do, you start to lose your sense of identity. Or it doesn't develop in the first place. This is common in people that do not know what they want to do in life. You may not even know what you like to do.

The Shadow Everyman can also manifest as anxiety. When you are not being True to your Self, the unconscious aspect of your personality will make you feel uncomfortable.

Denying yourself the things you want to do in life takes away the things that you need to grow emotionally and spiritually. As you get older, this will manifest as restlessness and an overwhelming desire to differentiate yourself from your friends.

CULTIVATE YOUR SENSE OF RELATABILITY AND AUTHENTICITY

Here are some practical exercises that can help the Everyman archetype cultivate their sense of relatability and authenticity:

1. Practice active listening: Take the time to truly listen to the people in your life. This means giving them your full attention and being present in the moment. Ask questions and show genuine interest in their experiences and perspectives.

2. Share your own experiences: Share your own experiences and perspectives with others. Be open and honest about your thoughts and feelings, and don't be afraid to show vulnerability.

3. Connect with others: Connect with people from all walks of life. This could involve joining a club or group that interests you, attending community events or volunteering your time with a local organization.

4. Embrace your flaws: Recognize that nobody is perfect and embrace your own imperfections. This can help you cultivate a sense of authenticity and relatability with others.

5. Practice empathy: Put yourself in other people's shoes and try to see things from their perspective. This can help you cultivate a sense of understanding and connection with those around you.

By practicing active listening, sharing your own experiences, connecting with others, embracing your flaws, and practicing empathy, you can develop the skills and qualities you need to be a relatable and authentic presence in all aspects of your life.

AFFIRMATIONS FOR THE EVERYMAN ARCHETYPE

- I am relatable and approachable to others.

- I am capable of adapting to any situation.

- I am a hard worker and dedicated to my goals.

- I am authentic and true to myself.

- I am able to find joy and humor in everyday situations.

- I am deserving of success and recognition.

- I am part of a larger community and have a place in the world.

- I am a good listener and friend to those around me.

- I am resourceful and able to problem-solve.

- I am humble and grateful for what I have

PROMPTS FOR THE EVERYMAN ARCHETYPE

What are some everyday actions you can take to be a positive and helpful presence in your community?

How can you cultivate a sense of humility and approachability in your interactions with others?

What kind of hobbies or interests can you pursue to connect with others and build relationships?

How can you use your relatable and approachable nature to create a sense of camaraderie and teamwork in your personal and professional life?

What kind of experiences or challenges have shaped your identity as an Everyman, and how can you use those experiences to connect with others?

What are some ways you can practice active listening and empathy to better understand the perspectives of those around you?

How can you use your natural inclination towards collaboration and teamwork to create positive change in your community or workplace?

What kind of leadership qualities can you develop to inspire and motivate others?

How can you approach your personal and professional goals with a sense of flexibility and adaptability, in order to make progress despite setbacks and obstacles?

What kind of support systems can you rely on to help you navigate challenges and stay motivated?

How can you use your relatable and approachable nature to bring diverse groups of people together and foster a sense of inclusivity?

What are some ways you can use your experiences and insights to create a sense of shared purpose and vision among those around you?

How can you approach your work and personal relationships with a sense of authenticity and integrity, even in challenging or high-pressure situations?

What kind of education or training can you pursue to enhance your skills and knowledge as an Everyman?

How can you approach conflicts or disagreements with others with a sense of diplomacy and a willingness to find common ground?

What are some ways you can use your strengths as an Everyman to support and uplift those around you?

How can you use your relatable and approachable nature to build trust and rapport with others?

How can you balance your desire for social connection and collaboration with your need for personal time and self-care?

What kind of impact can you make in your community or workplace by embodying the values of hard work, empathy, and collaboration?

How can you use your position as an Everyman to amplify the voices and perspectives of those who may be overlooked or marginalized?

What has been the most difficult challenge or loss you've faced, and how have you coped with it?

THE EXPLORER ARCHETYPE

ALSO KNOWN AS
The Seeker, The Wanderer, The Adventurer

TALENT
Independence, self-reliance, and the ability to live in
the moment

CORE DESIRE
To experience a sense of freedom and find one's own
path

MAIN GOAL
To find fulfillment through adventure and discovery

MOTTO
Don't fence me in

FATAL FLAW
Aimlessness

ADDICTION
Freedom

The Explorer archetype is often associated with adventure, excitement, and the search for new experiences. The Explorer seeks to push boundaries and challenge themselves to discover new things. They are open-minded about trying out new things, never content with boxing themselves in.

Awakened often during adolescence, the Explorer begins to separate from their guardian(s) and seek their distinct identity. With a certain curiosity, they embark on a voyage of self-discovery and independence. This is why this archetype develops more frequently in people with inquisitive minds, since they are always in search of meaning. Without this archetype developed in a person, they will later become dissatisfied with their lives and lack of identity, and from there, an existential crisis may develop.

THE SHADOW EXPLORER ARCHETYPE

Because society forces us to conform to pre-determined norms, people do not feel the need to explore alternative options. We also tend to believe what we are told as children and grow up with subconscious programs that create limiting beliefs, false truths and destructive habits. This is why the Explorer archetype is often one that remains repressed in adults and thus surfaces frequently in shadow behavior.

This also accounts for why pop music and mediocre TV shows are the norms for most people. If you settle for what you are handed on a plate without exploring alternative options, you will have a mediocre experience rather than a rich quality of life. A negative aspect of the Explorer is that you eventually feel unfulfilled, become restless and feel the need to change your circumstances. Individuals that have not developed a hero archetype by middle-age will typically undergo a mid-life crisis in search of an identity. If you are developing the Explorer aspect of your inner-hero, you probably need to make these changes.

Unless you reject societal norms, you will be molded into a sculpture created by other people. You will not be an individual with your own identity or independence; so, subsequently, you will feel lost and unfulfilled. When this happens, the True Self rebels and the Explorer archetype projects on to the ego.

The shadow explorer can also appear in destructive ways as there is a recklessness that can come with a desire for adventure. This can lead to taking unnecessary risks or not taking proper precautions, which can have negative consequences. For example, you may take an interest in drugs to escape the monotony and mundane nature of life. So long as the Explorer remains repressed, you will become addicted to whatever drives your motivation. An urge to do something dangerous for the adrenaline rush, the search for excitement and obsessive ambitions are all attributes of the seeker looking for something fulfilling.

The Explorer energy can also give you an irrational fear that you are missing out on something, so you often feel agitated and restless. You, therefore, flit from one thing to the next and never actually finish or accomplish anything.

On the other hand, if this energy is a dominant force in your psyche, you run the risk of never settling down, starting a family and finding stability.

Sometimes you need to appreciate what you do have and adopt the cliche: the journey is part of the destination.

A positive manifestation of the shadow is the urge to leave a job or a relationship that is not working for you. Sometimes, the situations you get trapped in are because of the conforming nature of the inner-child. The Explorer compels you to find your own path and mold your own identity.

Unless you develop the Explorer archetype, you will not mature or experience a rich quality of life. However, sometimes you need to call on the other attributes of the hero archetype – the hero and the lover.

CULTIVATE YOUR SENSE OF CURIOSITY AND ADVENTURE

Here are some practical exercises that can help the Explorer archetype cultivate their sense of curiosity and adventure:

1. Try something new: Step outside of your comfort zone. This could be as simple as trying a new food or taking a different route to work, or as adventurous as taking a solo trip to a new city or country.

2. Engage in physical activity: Get moving and engage in different physical activities. This could involve going for a hike, trying a new sport or fitness class or simply taking a walk in a new area.

3. Keep a travel journal: Document your travels and adventures in a travel journal. This can help you remember your experiences and reflect on what you've learned from them.

4. Learn a new skill: Challenge yourself to learn a new skill or hobby. This could involve learning a new language, taking up painting or photography or learning to play a musical instrument.

5. Connect with nature: Spend time in nature and take in the beauty of the world around you. Go for a hike, take a walk in the park or simply sit outside and observe the natural world. This can help you cultivate a sense of wonder and appreciation for the world around you.

By trying new things, engaging in physical activity, keeping a travel journal, learning a new skill, and connecting with nature, you can develop the skills and qualities you need to be an adventurous and curious explorer in all aspects of your life.

AFFIRMATIONS FOR THE EXPLORER ARCHETYPE

- I am adventurous and curious about the world.

- I have the courage to take risks and try new things.

- I am capable of overcoming obstacles and challenges.

- I am open to new experiences and perspectives.

- I am deserving of freedom and independence.

- I trust in my instincts and intuition.

- I am constantly learning and growing as a person.

- I am connected to nature and the world around me.

- I am a trailblazer and pathfinder for others.

- I am bold and fearless in the face of the unknown.

PROMPTS FOR THE EXPLORER ARCHETYPE

What new activities or experiences can you try to challenge yourself and expand your horizons?

How can you incorporate a sense of adventure and discovery into your daily routine?

What kind of travel destinations or outdoor activities interest you, and how can you plan to explore them?

What are some ways you can cultivate a sense of curiosity and wonder in your approach to life?

How can you use your exploratory nature to connect with people from diverse backgrounds and cultures?

What kind of physical challenges can you set for yourself to push your limits and build resilience?

How can you use your love of exploration to develop a deeper appreciation for the natural world?

What kind of risks or uncertainties are you willing to embrace in order to pursue your passions and goals?

How can you use your exploratory mindset to generate creative ideas and solutions?

What kind of learning opportunities can you seek out to expand your knowledge and skills?

How can you approach setbacks and failures as opportunities for growth and learning?

What kind of support systems can you rely on to help you overcome challenges and obstacles?

How can you use your exploratory nature to break out of routine and bring new energy to your work and personal life?

What kind of experiences or challenges have shaped your identity as an Explorer, and how can you use those experiences to inspire others?

How can you approach your personal and professional goals with a sense of optimism and a willingness to take calculated risks?

What are some ways you can use your love of exploration to inspire others to pursue their passions and dreams?

How can you cultivate a sense of adaptability and flexibility in your approach to life, in order to navigate unexpected changes or challenges?

What kind of outdoor or physical activities can you engage in to relieve stress and promote mental and emotional wellbeing?

How can you use your exploratory mindset to identify opportunities for positive change in your community or workplace?

What kind of connections or relationships can you build through your love of exploration and discovery?

What is one question or mystery that has always fascinated you, and how have you sought answers or insights about it?

THE LOVER ARCHETYPE

ALSO KNOWN AS
The Romantic, The Partner, The Friend

TALENT
Passion, warmth, and the ability to make others feel
special

CORE DESIRE
To experience intimacy and connect with others on a
deep level

MAIN GOAL
To experience intimacy and bliss

MOTTO
You're the only one

Fatal flaw
Co-dependency

ADDICTION
Pleasure

The Lover archetype allows you to love yourself in a healthy fashion and, consequently, develop the ability to love others as well. You come to value honesty and affection. You become comfortable with yourself and find happiness in your relationships with others, which you take joy in cultivating into long-term ones.

You start to understand what it is you like and dislike and take control of your passions. You come to appreciate the world around you and enjoy them exquisitely through your senses. You feel a deep connection with the world around you and start to live life as an independent creature.

The Lover archetype represents passion, desire and emotional connection. It is often associated with romantic love but can also represent the desire for emotional connection in other forms of relationships. The Lover seeks to create deep emotional connections with others and experience the depths of human emotion.

Integrating the Lover to form your overall coherent self is vital for understanding life and pursuing your interests and passions. Empathy is a tool you should develop if you are to grow the Lover in you.

THE SHADOW LOVER ARCHETYPE

The shadow lover, like any other shadow, is born from the repression of aspects of itself. Owing to the patriarchal order or certain religions common in the world, men generally repress their Lover archetype. Abandonment during childhood also sparks the shadow lover into life. The shadow lover loses touch with themselves and their emotions, and thus hinders the Lover archetype from sprouting forth.

The shadow of the lover is the obsession and possessiveness that can come with a desire for emotional connection. This can lead to unhealthy relationships or a lack of respect for boundaries.

They start to feel empty, devoid of any passion or interest in anything. A lack of self-love develops that eventually prevents them from forming any meaningful relationship. Finally, the shadow lover moves down a winding road of destructive behaviors to their doom.

As their Lover archetype has been repressed, they also become dissatisfied with every experience they pass through, and thus they begin to seek out thrills or an object to fill the void of love in them. This can result in tendencies such as substance abuse, promiscuity, wasteful spending or getting into toxic relationships.

The thought that they cannot love or don't deserve to be loved by others is another source of the shadow lover. This typically leads the person to project these thoughts onto others and any new relationship they find themselves in, thereby sabotaging it.

For this shadow, it is necessary to awaken the explorer in you and embark on a journey of self-journey. You have to discover, or rediscover, yourself.

CULTIVATE YOUR SENSE OF PASSION AND CONNECTION

Here are some practical exercises that can help the Lover archetype cultivate their sense of passion and connection:

1. Practice gratitude: Take the time to appreciate the people and things you love in your life. Write down a list of things you're grateful for and make an effort to express your appreciation to the people who matter most to you.

2. Connect with others: Cultivate strong, meaningful relationships with the people in your life. Take the time to show love and affection towards your loved ones, and be there for them when they need you.

3. Engage your senses: Pay attention to your senses and engage in activities that bring you pleasure. This could involve listening to your favorite music, enjoying your favorite foods or taking a relaxing bath.

4. Express yourself creatively: Find creative ways to express your love and passion. This could involve writing poetry, painting or even cooking a delicious meal for someone you care about.

5. Practice self-love: Take care of yourself and practice self-love. This could involve taking time to relax, treating yourself to something you enjoy or simply taking a break when you need it.

By practicing gratitude, connecting with others, engaging your senses, expressing yourself creatively and practicing self-love, you can develop the skills and qualities you need to be a passionate and loving presence in all aspects of your life.

AFFIRMATIONS FOR THE LOVER ARCHETYPE

- I am deserving of love and affection.
- I am able to give and receive love freely.
- I am passionate and expressive in my relationships.
- I am worthy of being pursued and desired.
- I am able to form deep and meaningful connections with others.

- I am open to new and diverse experiences of love.

- I embrace sensuality and pleasure in my life.

- I radiate beauty and attractiveness.

- I am confident and secure in my relationships.

- I am a lover of life and all its experiences.

PROMPTS FOR THE LOVER ARCHETYPE

What qualities and values are most important to you in your personal and romantic relationships?

How can you cultivate deeper intimacy and emotional connection with your partner or loved ones?

What kind of creative expression or artistic pursuits resonate with your emotional and sensual nature?

How can you use your love of beauty and aesthetics to enhance your physical surroundings and environment?

What kind of self-care practices can you engage in to nourish your emotional and physical wellbeing?

How can you use your empathic and intuitive nature to better understand and support the needs of those around you?

What kind of healthy boundaries can you set in order to maintain your own emotional and physical health?

How can you use your capacity for love and compassion to promote positive social change and justice?

What kind of personal growth and development can you pursue in order to enhance your ability to give and receive love?

How can you balance your own needs and desires with the needs and desires of those you love and care for?

What kind of romantic or sensual experiences do you desire, and how can you make them a reality in your life?

How can you use your love of beauty and aesthetics to inspire and uplift those around you?

What kind of self-reflection or introspection can you engage in to better understand your own emotional needs and desires?

How can you use your emotional intelligence and sensitivity to build stronger and more meaningful relationships?

What kind of communication skills can you develop in order to express your feelings and desires effectively and compassionately?

How can you use your love of beauty and aesthetics to contribute to positive change in the world?

What kind of creative outlets or hobbies can you pursue to connect with your emotional and sensual nature?

How can you use your capacity for love and empathy to create a more compassionate and connected world?

What kind of values and beliefs are most important to you in your personal and professional life, and how can you align them with your capacity for love and compassion?

How can you use your emotional and intuitive nature to inspire and guide others towards greater love, connection, and wellbeing?

What is one experience or relationship that has taught you the most about love and connection, and how has it shaped you?

THE HERO ARCHETYPE

ALSO KNOWN AS
The Warrior, The Champion, The Athlete

TALENT
Courage, perseverance, and the ability to take risks

CORE DESIRE
To prove oneself through acts of bravery and heroism

MAIN GOAL
To prove oneself through courageous acts

MOTTO
Where there's a will, there's a way

FATAL FLAW
Hubris

ADDICTION
Winning

The Hero archetype represents bravery, courage and strength. It is often associated with the desire to overcome obstacles and achieve greatness. The Hero seeks to make a positive difference in the world and stand up for what is right.

The Hero is usually characterized by courage and motivation. The world is filled with challenges and the archetype of the Hero is what lets one take risks, pursuing what they believe is right. They also try to help others as well, guided by the same stimulus common to heroes found in stories and myths. They are typically energized by a will that compels them to face their fears, and persevere in whatever activity they engage in, regardless of the number of failures they face.

This archetype is an invaluable catalyst for learning new things through your experiences, and it provides one with the courage to keep on moving, despite the hardships.

THE SHADOW HERO ARCHETYPE

Archetypical energy that appears on the shadow side of the hero is a willingness to fight the good fight but for the wrong cause. This can lead you to defend your values and actions or remain loyal to someone, even when the facts and motivations are not in your best interests or contribute to the greater good.

The shadow side to the hero character is often found in individuals that had authoritarian parent(s) or teachers, especially if you felt your behavior and achievements were being harshly criticized, or if they suffered failure early in life.

But it can just as easily originate from infanthood when you were denied or refused something you wanted and developed a program that you are not worthy enough.

Until you recognize and acknowledge your actions do not serve your best interests or the interests of others, the shadow side of the warrior will keep prompting you to perform actions that create chaos.

The hero-warrior, although having outgrown the child, is still among the immature archetypes. The weakness is in failing to control your desires with rational thinking.

The shadow hero can also represent the desire for power and control, and it can manifest in negative behaviors such as aggression and violence. The negative Hero represents the part of us that wants to dominate and control others, and it is often associated with feelings of anger and resentment.

There may also be times when you feel vulnerable or dependent on others to make your decisions for you rather than voicing what you really want. A weak Hero will typically avoid taking an opportunity because it's easier to stay in your comfort zone.

An underdeveloped hero archetype will prompt you to shy away from challenges or lose your nerve during a contest. If you play a game of skill, the shadow archetype will give you the proverbial stage fright when you are in the jaws of victory.

Other times, though, you will act spontaneously without a plan. Here we see the naivety of the child that has not yet developed hero consciousness. Whereas spontaneity is a good way of developing the archetypes that constitute the Hero, other times it will leave you unprepared and floundering – so choose your moments wisely.

People that look to establish their sense of Self are on the path to expressing their uniqueness. There is a lingering feeling that you have to prove yourself and leave a mark on the world. The warrior can help you achieve your goals but unless the positive aspects of this energy are developed, the hero archetype is destructive and harmful.

This act of defiance is the explorer or outlaw archetype which are essential aspects of the hero. It can often surface in people in their 40's that decide to leave the corporate world and set up their own business, design an innovative product or develop an innovative form of creative work.

CULTIVATE YOUR SENSE OF STRENGTH AND COURAGE

Here are some practical exercises that can help the Hero archetype cultivate their sense of strength and courage:

1. Set goals and take action: Set challenging goals for yourself and take action to achieve them. This could involve setting fitness or career goals or tackling a project that you've been putting off.

2. Practice self-discipline: Cultivate self-discipline and self-control in all aspects of your life. This could involve sticking to a regular exercise routine, eating a healthy diet or practicing good time management.

3. Face your fears: Confront your fears head-on and develop the courage to face them. This could involve taking on a challenge that scares you or simply speaking up when you feel uncomfortable.

4. Practice mindfulness: Cultivate a sense of mindfulness and awareness in your daily life. This could involve practicing meditation or yoga, or simply taking a few minutes each day to reflect on your thoughts and feelings.

5. Serve others: Develop a sense of service and purpose by volunteering your time to help others. This could involve working with a local charity or non-profit organization, or simply helping out a friend or family member in need.

By setting goals and taking action, practicing self-discipline, facing your fears, practicing mindfulness, and serving others, you can develop the skills and qualities you need to be a strong and courageous warrior in all aspects of your life.

AFFIRMATIONS FOR THE HERO ARCHETYPE

- I am strong and capable of overcoming any obstacle in my path.

- I embrace challenges as opportunities for growth and transformation.

- I trust my instincts and make decisions with confidence.

- I am resilient and can handle anything that comes my way.

- I am a leader and inspire others to be their best selves.

- I am courageous and willing to face my fears head-on.

- I have the power to create change in my life and in the world around me.

- I am disciplined and dedicated to achieving my goals.

- I am driven by my values and principles, and stand up for what I believe in.

- I am a warrior, and I will fight for what is right with honor and integrity.

PROMPTS FOR THE HERO ARCHETYPE

What kind of goals and objectives are most important to you, and how can you pursue them with courage and determination?

How can you use your physical and mental strength to overcome challenges and obstacles in your life?

What kind of physical exercise or training can you engage in to maintain your strength and resilience?

How can you use your leadership skills to inspire and motivate others to pursue their own goals and objectives?

What kind of challenges or obstacles have you overcome in the past, and how have they made you stronger?

How can you use your capacity for strategic thinking and problem-solving to overcome challenges in your personal and professional life?

What kind of values and beliefs are most important to you, and how can you uphold them with integrity and honor?

How can you use your inner fire and passion to fuel your pursuit of excellence and success?

What kind of rituals or practices can you engage in to connect with your inner warrior spirit?

How can you use your sense of justice and fairness to promote positive change and protect those who are vulnerable?

What kind of communication skills can you develop in order to assert your needs and boundaries effectively and assertively?

How can you use your strength and resilience to bounce back from setbacks and failures?

What kind of leadership skills can you develop in order to inspire and guide others towards success and growth?

How can you use your sense of purpose and mission to stay focused and motivated in pursuit of your goals?

What kind of discipline and self-control can you cultivate in order to maintain your physical and mental strength?

How can you use your courage and determination to overcome fears and doubts?

What kind of teamwork and collaboration skills can you develop in order to achieve greater success and impact?

How can you use your capacity for risk-taking and adventure to pursue new opportunities and experiences?

What kind of values and beliefs can you cultivate in order to stay true to your warrior spirit and purpose?

How can you use your strength and power to make a positive impact in the world and contribute to the greater good?

What is one fear or limiting belief that holds you back from achieving your goals, and how can you overcome it?

THE SAGE ARCHETYPE

ALSO KNOWN AS
The Scholar, The Thinker, The Expert

TALENT
Wisdom, intelligence, and objectivity

CORE DESIRE
To seek truth and knowledge in all things

MAIN GOAL
To seek the truth and knowledge

MOTTO
The truth will set you free

FATAL FLAW
Analysis paralysis

ADDICTION
Information

The Sage is nearly identical with the Magician archetype, with the difference being that the magician applies his skills better after receiving wisdom from the Sage. The Sage brings out the full potential of the magician. It is the matured version of the magician without any illusions and possessing complete control over their emotions. They are able to detach themselves from their emotions and obtain wisdom.

The Sage archetype represents wisdom, knowledge and understanding; it is often associated with the pursuit of knowledge and the desire to understand the world around us. It prompts us to seek to gain knowledge and understanding in order to make sense of the world and help others.

Picture the Sage as the wise old man you find in myths and fairytales, a force that drives you to seek out knowledge to fill the void the magician has. The Sage helps you create better life strategies and perceive things around you with perfect clarity. It is like August Rodin's statue, a profound thinker, constantly philosophizing on their experiences of the world, and trying to understand what truth in this planet of ours really is. But because of this overly ponderous mind, the Sage tends to think without ever acting. The countless ideas and epiphanies that arise remain buried in their mind, without the support of the magician.

It is important to merge the qualities of the Sage with that of either the explorer or hero/warrior. You have to act for your knowledge to mean anything. It is your king that will command the warrior or explorer to apply the wisdom of the Sage and bring it to reality.

THE SHADOW SAGE ARCHETYPE

The shadow sage, if left unchecked, can come to dominate and guide the shadow ruler in his reign of tyranny. The shadow sage starts to lack patience with the people around them, especially those they feel aren't equal to them intellectually. They become stubborn and nearly impossible to deal with or reason with; as a result, a majority of people with this quality tend to alienate themselves from society at large. Following this path, they are often immersed in illusions — a world of brilliant dreams — that will go unfulfilled.

The shadow sage represents the desire for knowledge and understanding at any cost, and it can manifest in negative behaviors such as intellectual arrogance and elitism. It also represents the part of us that wants to be superior to others, which is often associated with feelings of isolation and loneliness. This alienation can further lead to a disintegration of empathy.

Most of the time, the shadow sage is manifested due to constant dismissal of their ideas while growing up. Their drive for action becomes extinguished and a fear of expressing themselves before people starts to germinate, so out of arrogance, they dismiss others first. They become the ones that are always right.

In order to grow, it is important to cultivate the feminine principle within us and develop a balance of our thoughts and emotions. We should integrate our heart with our minds and learn to empathize with other people. Moreover, it is also necessary to adopt an objective stance when watching the things around us. Learn to observe the things around you without taking a preference for any of them, and in this way, grow a higher wisdom.

The Zen master Takuan Soho once wrote, "When facing a single tree, if you look at a single one of its red leaves, you will not see all the others. When the eye is not set on any one leaf, and you face the tree with nothing at all in mind, any number of leaves are visible to the eye without limit. But if a single leaf holds the eye, it will be as if the remaining leaves were not there." Hence, for complete self-development, you need to learn to see the bigger picture and avoid all illusions.

CULTIVATE YOUR SENSE OF WISDOM AND KNOWLEDGE

Here are some practical exercises that can help the Sage archetype cultivate their sense of wisdom and knowledge:

1. Read and learn: Cultivate a habit of reading and learning. Set aside time each day to read books, articles, or other sources of information that interest you.

2. Seek out new experiences: Try new things and explore new ideas. Travel to new places, take classes on subjects that interest you or simply try a new hobby or activity.

3. Practice critical thinking: Develop your critical thinking skills by questioning assumptions, evaluating evidence and examining different perspectives.

4. Teach and share knowledge: Share your knowledge and wisdom with others. This could involve teaching a class, mentoring a younger person or simply sharing what you've learned with friends and family.

5. Reflect and meditate: Take time to reflect on your thoughts and feelings, and practice mindfulness or meditation. This can help you cultivate a deeper sense of self-awareness and understanding.

By reading and learning, seeking out new experiences, practicing critical thinking, teaching and sharing knowledge, and reflecting and meditating, you can develop the skills and qualities you need to be a wise and knowledgeable Sage in all aspects of your life.

AFFIRMATIONS FOR THE SAGE ARCHETYPE

- I am wise and seek knowledge and understanding in all areas of my life.

- I trust my intuition and insights to guide me in making wise decisions.

- I am a lifelong learner and constantly seek to expand my knowledge and awareness.

- I am a teacher and share my wisdom and insights with others to help them grow.

- I value critical thinking and approach problems with an open and analytical mind.

- I am patient and take time to reflect and consider all options before making decisions.

- I am a master of my emotions and use my intellect to stay calm and rational in difficult situations.

- I am curious and enjoy exploring new ideas and concepts.

- I am a visionary and can see the bigger picture, beyond the immediate circumstances.

- I am a sage, and I use my wisdom to create positive change in my life and in the world around me.

PROMPTS FOR THE SAGE ARCHETYPE

What kind of knowledge and wisdom do you seek, and how can you pursue it with an open mind and a thirst for understanding?

How can you use your capacity for critical thinking and analysis to gain a deeper understanding of the world around you?

What kind of insights and ideas can you share with others to help them gain a deeper understanding of themselves and their place in the world?

How can you use your love of learning and exploration to expand your horizons and explore new ideas and perspectives?

What kind of practices or rituals can you engage in to cultivate a sense of inner wisdom and clarity?

How can you use your capacity for reflection and introspection to gain a deeper understanding of your own beliefs and values?

What kind of intellectual pursuits or projects can you engage in to satisfy your thirst for knowledge and understanding?

How can you use your ability to communicate complex ideas and concepts in simple, accessible language to help others learn and grow?

What kind of creative or artistic pursuits can you engage in to explore new ideas and express your inner wisdom and insights?

How can you use your love of books and literature to gain new insights and perspectives on the human experience?

What kind of mentorship or teaching can you offer to others who seek your wisdom and guidance?

How can you use your capacity for analysis and synthesis to make connections between seemingly disparate fields or ideas?

What kind of intellectual or philosophical debates can you engage in to challenge your own beliefs and sharpen your thinking?

How can you use your sense of curiosity and wonder to explore the mysteries of the universe and the human experience?

What kind of contemplative practices or meditation can you engage in to cultivate a sense of inner peace and wisdom?

How can you use your capacity for abstract thinking and problem-solving to tackle complex issues and find innovative solutions?

What kind of intellectual communities or networks can you engage in to connect with others who share your thirst for knowledge and wisdom?

How can you use your insights and knowledge to make a positive impact in the world and contribute to the greater good?

What kind of ethical or moral principles can you cultivate to guide your intellectual pursuits and actions in the world?

How can you use your inner wisdom and insight to lead others towards greater understanding and enlightenment?

What is one lesson or insight that you've learned from a difficult or challenging experience, and how has it informed your wisdom?

THE MAGICIAN ARCHETYPE

ALSO KNOWN AS
The Visionary, The Alchemist, The Shaman

TALENT
Creativity, imagination, and the ability to transform
reality

CORE DESIRE
To create something extraordinary and make dreams
a reality

MAIN GOAL
To transform reality and make dreams come true

MOTTO
Anything is possible

FATAL FLAW
Manipulation

ADDICTION
Control

The Magician archetype serves as the bridge to creation. It represents transformation, change and the power of the unseen. This archetype is often associated with the desire to create change through the use of unseen forces or energies that are expressed as powerful intuitive thoughts and feelings.

The Magician, sometimes called the sorcerer or wizard, seeks to create change in the world through the power of their own will. They can turn the most mundane thing into something extraordinary. They also display a heightened perception of reality and with the knowledge they constantly gather, they use it to shape the world around them.

THE SHADOW MAGICIAN ARCHETYPE

The shadow of the magician is the manipulation and deception that can come with a desire for power. This can lead to using others for personal gain or using dark forces to achieve goals. Although the Magician's energy enables you to see more alternatives, you may not always be satisfied with the options you have and feel there is a better option. This will leave you feeling unsatisfied with what you've got. Hence, they start to crave more.

Your superior knowledge can also quickly leave you dissatisfied with the company of other people. For the Magician that has mastered the art of detachment, this can pose problems with your willingness to connect with people. You may even cut people out of your life. Doing so can starve you of emotional nutrition. When the Magician energy is unbalanced, you may also tend to analyze your emotions intellectually rather than experiencing the feeling.

You may not be interested in material possessions, but as a result, you might take it too far and deny yourself the smaller pleasures in life enjoyed by the lover archetype. What is important during individuation is finding that balance that allows the archetypes to integrate fully.

Another shadow energy the magician possesses is being overly critical – even to the part of being paranoid. Because the Magician is highly intuitive, a fearful ego that associates with this archetype will skew your perception.

Whereas skepticism can serve to protect you at times, it can also prevent you from experiencing a richer quality of life. In such circumstances, you need to call upon the energy of the warrior in order to integrate both archetypes into the King.

CULTIVATE YOUR SENSE OF TRANSFORMATION AND MANIFESTATION

Here are some practical exercises that can help the Magician archetype cultivate their sense of transformation and manifestation:

1. Practice visualization: Visualize your goals and dreams as if they have already come true. This can help you manifest your desires and bring them into reality.

2. Explore your intuition: Cultivate a sense of intuition and trust your inner guidance. This could involve practicing meditation, journaling or simply taking time to reflect on your thoughts and feelings.

3. Experiment with different perspectives: Explore different perspectives and ways of looking at the world. This could involve reading books, watching documentaries or simply engaging in conversations with people who have different viewpoints.

4. Cultivate creativity: Explore your creative side and find ways to express yourself through art, music, writing or other creative outlets.

5. Connect with nature: Spend time in nature and connect with the natural world. This can help you tap into the power of the universe and feel more connected to the world around you.

By practicing visualization, exploring your intuition, experimenting with different perspectives, cultivating creativity, and connecting with nature, you can develop the skills and qualities you need to be a powerful magician in all aspects of your life.

AFFIRMATIONS FOR THE MAGICIAN ARCHETYPE

- I am a powerful creator and can manifest my desires into reality.

- I trust in the Universe to guide me towards my highest good.

- I am open to receiving abundance in all areas of my life.

- I am connected to my inner wisdom and use it to make decisions that align with my purpose.

- I believe in the power of visualization and use it to manifest my goals and dreams.

- I am intuitive and trust my inner guidance to lead me towards my path.

- I am a master of transformation and can turn any negative experience into a positive one.

- I am aligned with the flow of life and embrace change as an opportunity for growth and evolution.

- I am connected to the divine and use my spiritual practices to elevate my consciousness.

- I am a Magician, and I use my powers to create a world filled with love, joy, and abundance.

PROMPTS FOR THE MAGICIAN ARCHETYPE

What kind of inner transformation or personal growth do you seek, and how can you use your magic to facilitate this process?

How can you use your power of imagination to envision a new reality and manifest it in your life and the world around you?

What kind of practices or rituals can you engage in to cultivate a sense of inner magic and intuition?

How can you use your capacity for creativity and innovation to bring new ideas and solutions to old problems?

What kind of symbols or metaphors can you use to tap into your subconscious mind and unlock your full potential?

How can you use your magical abilities to heal yourself and others on a physical, emotional, and spiritual level?

What kind of transformational experiences or journeys can you engage in to deepen your understanding of the mysteries of life and the universe?

How can you use your capacity for illusion and sleight of hand to entertain and delight others?

What kind of magical tools or objects can you create or use to enhance your practice and connect with your inner magic?

How can you use your ability to see beyond the surface level of things to gain a deeper understanding of the hidden truths and mysteries of life?

What kind of spiritual practices or traditions can you engage in to connect with higher realms of consciousness and wisdom?

How can you use your magical abilities to inspire and uplift others, and help them tap into their own inner magic?

What kind of inner demons or shadow aspects do you need to confront in order to fully harness your magical powers?

How can you use your capacity for symbolism and metaphor to communicate complex ideas and concepts in a simple and accessible way?

What kind of magical beings or entities can you connect with to gain wisdom and guidance on your spiritual journey?

How can you use your magical abilities to cultivate a sense of wonder and awe in your daily life and experiences?

What kind of transformative practices or experiences can you engage in to tap into your full potential as a magical being?

How can you use your magical powers to bring light to the darkness and bring positive change to the world around you?

What kind of spiritual or mystical traditions can you draw inspiration from to deepen your practice and expand your understanding of the universe?

How can you use your inner magic to cultivate a sense of unity and interconnectedness with all beings and the universe as a whole?

What is one goal or transformation that you've achieved through sheer willpower and determination, and how did you do it?

THE JESTER ARCHETYPE

ALSO KNOWN AS

The Entertainer, The Comedian, The Fool

TALENT

Humor, playfulness, and the ability to bring joy to others

CORE DESIRE

To have fun and enjoy life to the fullest

MAIN GOAL

To make others laugh and enjoy life

MOTTO

You only live once

FATAL FLAW

Frivolity

ADDICTION

Fun

The Jester archetype, also known as the trickster, represents humor, playfulness and the desire to create joy and laughter. It is often associated with the desire to make others happy and create a sense of lightness/joy in the world through humor and playfulness.

The presence of the Jester, with its free spirit and pleasure-seeking habits, liberates one from the stressful monotony of everyday life. They are energized with a creativity that lets them see the world in a novel perspective, and gives them a knack for laughing at the boring way the world operates. They have a thinking pattern that deviates from the box of normal reasoning and lets them achieve things people thought originally impossible.

THE SHADOW JESTER ARCHETYPE

The shadow of the jester is the use of humor to mask pain or hide true emotions. This can lead to a lack of authenticity or a lack of empathy for others. The Jester archetype is most dominant in people that are dishonest with themselves.

It represents the desire for chaos and destruction, and it can manifest in negative behaviors such as deception and manipulation. The negative Jester represents the part of us that wants to cause trouble and disrupt the status quo, and it is often associated with feelings of anxiety and insecurity.

These are symptoms of an immature mind that has not outgrown the childish behavior which makes the Jester archetype such an adorable character. When permitted to project too often, the trickster can become annoying. You will find yourself caught in two minds, confused by the crossroads you encounter, make jokes in inappropriate moments and feel sexually rampant.

If you observe what happens and how you feel when the shadow trickster is at play, you can release trapped emotions that are buried deep in your subconscious.

Despite its mad qualities, the Jester archetype has the power to create order out of pure chaos and are hence indispensable to you.

CULTIVATE YOUR SENSE OF HUMOR, SPONTANEITY, AND JOY

Here are some practical exercises that can help the Jester archetype cultivate their sense of humor, spontaneity and joy:

1. Embrace playfulness: Cultivate a sense of playfulness in your daily life. This could involve playing games, telling jokes or simply engaging in activities that bring you joy.

2. Practice improvisation: Learn to think on your feet and improvise in different situations. This could involve taking an improv class, participating in a group activity that requires quick thinking or simply challenging yourself to come up with creative solutions on the spot.

3. Find the humor in difficult situations: Develop a sense of humor that allows you to find the lightness in difficult situations. This could involve reframing challenges as opportunities for growth or simply learning to laugh at yourself when things don't go as planned.

4. Connect with others: Use humor and wit to connect with others and build relationships. This could involve sharing a funny story, making a witty comment or simply being willing to laugh and have fun with others.

5. Create and perform: Find creative outlets for your humor and spontaneity. This could involve writing jokes or stories, creating comedy sketches or performing in front of an audience.

By embracing playfulness, practicing improvisation, finding the humor in difficult situations, connecting with others, and creating and performing, you can develop the skills and qualities you need to be a joyful and playful jester in all aspects of your life.

AFFIRMATIONS FOR THE JESTER ARCHETYPE

- I embrace humor and playfulness in my life, and I approach challenges with a light heart.

- I am free to express myself creatively, without fear of judgment or criticism.

- I am comfortable in my own skin and find joy in being my true, authentic self.

- I choose to see the positive in every situation and find laughter in even the most challenging moments.

- I am a source of light and inspiration to those around me, bringing joy and happiness wherever I go.

- I am free to let go of expectations and simply enjoy the present moment.

- I use my humor and wit to diffuse tension and bring people together in times of conflict.

- I am able to find the balance between seriousness and levity, allowing me to navigate life's ups and downs with ease.

- I bring a unique perspective and energy to any situation, inspiring creativity and innovation.

- I am a Jester, and I use my humor and lightheartedness to bring joy and laughter into the world.

PROMPTS FOR THE JESTER ARCHETYPE

What is one thing you've always wanted to do but never had the courage to try?

Who is someone you admire for their sense of humor? Why?

How do you react when you feel stressed or overwhelmed?

What is your favorite childhood memory?

What is one thing you can do to bring more joy into your life?

If you could have any superpower, what would it be and why?

What is the funniest thing that has ever happened to you?

Who is someone you consider a mentor or role model? Why?

What is one thing you can do today to make someone else smile?

How do you deal with failure or setbacks?

What is your favorite form of self-expression (e.g. writing, drawing, singing)?

Who is someone you've lost touch with that you'd like to reconnect with? Why?

What is something you've always wanted to learn but never had the time or opportunity to do so?

Describe a time when you felt truly alive and joyful.

Who is someone in your life that you can always count on to make you laugh?

What is your go-to source of inspiration when you feel stuck or unmotivated?

What is one thing you can do to bring more humor and playfulness into your relationships?

Describe a situation where you used humor to diffuse a tense or difficult situation.

Who is someone you've always wanted to emulate or be like? Why?

What is one thing you can do to step out of your comfort zone and try something new or daring?

What is one thing that you take too seriously, and how can you bring a
sense of humor or playfulness to it?

THE OUTLAW ARCHETYPE

ALSO KNOWN AS
The Rebel, The Maverick, The Misfit

TALENT
Boldness, nonconformity, and the ability to challenge authority

CORE DESIRE
To break the rules and find freedom from constraints

MAIN GOAL
To rebel against the norm and authority

MOTTO
Rules are made to be broken

FATAL FLAW
Self-destructiveness

ADDICTION
Adrenaline

The Outlaw or rebel archetype represents rebellion, nonconformity and independence. It is often associated with the desire to challenge authority and break free from societal norms. The Outlaw is outspoken and seeks to create their own path and live life on their own terms, entirely unafraid to pursue radical approaches and make daring decisions.

They are capable of seeing beyond appearances and perceive the truth in the world around them, and this is what drives them to courageously rebel against those systems they feel are oppressive. The rules are broken in order to gain a sense of independence and identity.

THE SHADOW OUTLAW ARCHETYPE

The shadow of the outlaw is the disregard for rules and laws that can come with a desire for rebellion. This can lead to criminal behavior or a lack of concern for the well-being of others. Endowed with courage from the Outlaw archetypical energy, you may try and bring about the change by doing something stupid that has not been thought through.

When the ego associates with the shadow side of the rebel archetype, you typically complain about things rather than making a change in themselves to change it. In this instance, the Outlaw archetype is not developed and the positive energies are still submerged in the unconscious. The energy has emerged as an idea but the individual has not found the courage to explore the matter for a solution or enact a change.

On the flip side, to successfully integrate the Outlaw archetype, you must be prepared to make changes logically and adapt to new ways of life. This means integrating the traits of the father archetype into your Self-ego axis. The positive warrior archetype is also essential as, in its fullness, it gives you the power to make the right decision even if it means walking away.

CULTIVATE YOUR SENSE OF REBELLION, FREEDOM, AND INDEPENDENCE

Here are some practical exercises that can help the Outlaw archetype cultivate their sense of rebellion, freedom and independence:

1. Challenge authority: Identify areas in your life where you feel restricted or oppressed by authority figures, rules or societal norms, then find ways to rebel against them in a constructive way. This could involve questioning rules, standing up for your rights or simply expressing your opinions and beliefs.

2. Explore alternative lifestyles: Embrace alternative lifestyles that challenge the status quo and provide a sense of freedom and independence. This could involve traveling, living off the grid or simply exploring different subcultures and communities.

3. Take calculated risks: Develop a sense of courage and willingness to take risks in pursuit of your goals and desires. This could involve starting your own business, taking up a new hobby or passion or simply challenging yourself to step outside your comfort zone.

4. Stand up for justice: Develop a strong sense of justice and stand up for what you believe is right, even if it goes against the norm or risks consequences. This could involve advocating for social causes, speaking out against injustices or simply standing up for those who are marginalized or oppressed.

5. Embrace your rebellious spirit: Celebrate your rebellious spirit and embrace your unique qualities and traits. This could involve expressing yourself through fashion, music or other forms of self-expression, or simply embracing your quirks and idiosyncrasies.

By challenging authority, exploring alternative lifestyles, taking calculated risks, standing up for justice, and embracing your rebellious spirit, you can develop the skills and qualities you need to be a powerful Outlaw in all aspects of your life.

AFFIRMATIONS FOR THE OUTLAW ARCHETYPE

- I am unafraid to challenge the status quo and fight against injustice and oppression.
- I am a rebel with a cause, using my power and influence to effect positive change in the world.
- I am confident in my own convictions and beliefs, even in the face of opposition or criticism.
- I am a champion of freedom and individuality, and I stand up for those who cannot stand up for themselves.
- I am able to think outside the box and see beyond the limits of convention and tradition.
- I am a force for change and progress, unafraid to take risks and break new ground.
- I am a true individual, refusing to be defined by society's expectations or limitations.
- I am a trailblazer, forging my own path and paving the way for others to follow.
- I am a rebel with a heart, using my power to uplift and empower the marginalized and oppressed.
- I am an Outlaw, and I embrace my role as a disruptor and agent of change in the world.

PROMPTS FOR THE OUTLAW ARCHETYPE

What is one societal norm that you have always questioned or challenged?

Who is someone you consider a rebel or iconoclast? Why?

What is one thing you've always wanted to do but felt was too risky or dangerous?

Describe a time when you felt like an outsider or rebelled against authority.

What is one issue or cause that you feel passionately about?

If you could live anywhere in the world, where would you go and why?

What is your favorite form of self-expression that may be considered unconventional or non-traditional?

Who is someone you admire for their courage or fearlessness? Why?

What is one thing you've done in the past that you're proud of, even if it went against societal norms or expectations?

Describe a time when you had to stand up for yourself or someone else against a perceived injustice.

What is one thing you can do to challenge the status quo in your personal or professional life?

Who is someone you know who embodies the Outlaw archetype? How do they inspire you?

What is one fear or limiting belief that you would like to overcome?

If you could be any fictional character, who would you be and why?

Describe a situation where you had to make a tough decision that went against what was expected of you.

Who is someone you've always wanted to confront or challenge? Why?

What is your favorite form of rebellion or defiance, either in your own life or in society at large?

Describe a time when you felt like an underdog and had to fight against the odds.

What is one rule or law that you've always felt was unjust or unnecessary?

What is one thing you can do to embrace your rebellious or nonconformist side?

What is one rule or convention that you've challenged or broken, and how did it liberate or empower you?

THE
SHADOW WORK
JOURNAL

Your Daily Companion to Wholeness and Freedom

Guided Prompts, Exercises, and Rituals to Deepen Self-Awareness, Spark Lasting Change, and Prevent Setbacks.

Samantha Jones

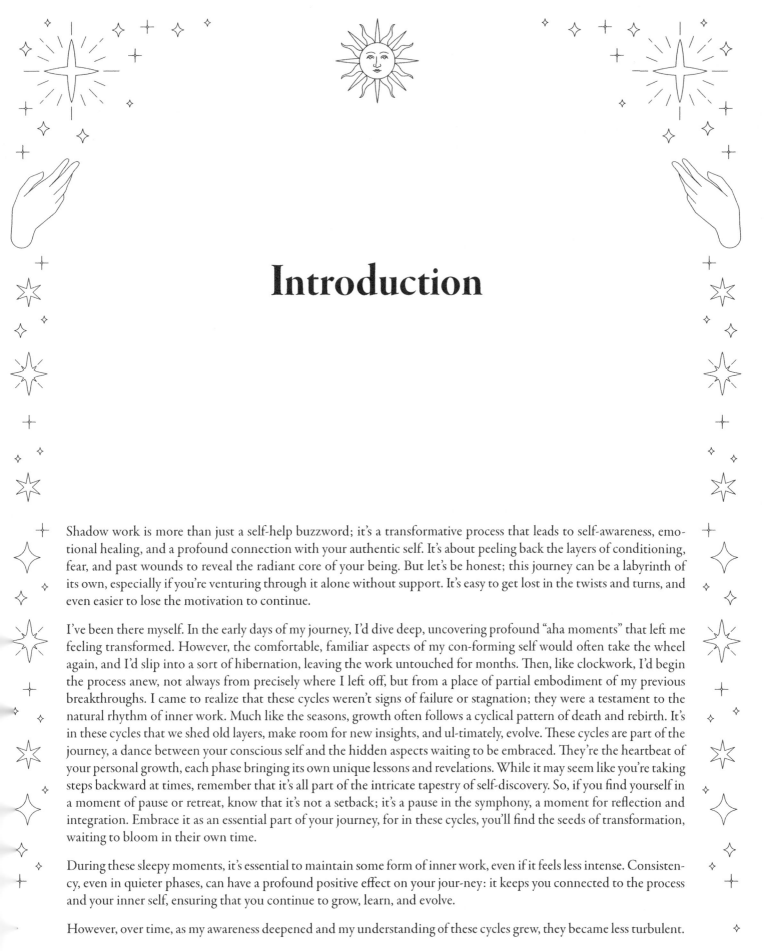

Introduction

Shadow work is more than just a self-help buzzword; it's a transformative process that leads to self-awareness, emotional healing, and a profound connection with your authentic self. It's about peeling back the layers of conditioning, fear, and past wounds to reveal the radiant core of your being. But let's be honest; this journey can be a labyrinth of its own, especially if you're venturing through it alone without support. It's easy to get lost in the twists and turns, and even easier to lose the motivation to continue.

I've been there myself. In the early days of my journey, I'd dive deep, uncovering profound "aha moments" that left me feeling transformed. However, the comfortable, familiar aspects of my con-forming self would often take the wheel again, and I'd slip into a sort of hibernation, leaving the work untouched for months. Then, like clockwork, I'd begin the process anew, not always from precisely where I left off, but from a place of partial embodiment of my previous breakthroughs. I came to realize that these cycles weren't signs of failure or stagnation; they were a testament to the natural rhythm of inner work. Much like the seasons, growth often follows a cyclical pattern of death and rebirth. It's in these cycles that we shed old layers, make room for new insights, and ul-timately, evolve. These cycles are part of the journey, a dance between your conscious self and the hidden aspects waiting to be embraced. They're the heartbeat of your personal growth, each phase bringing its own unique lessons and revelations. While it may seem like you're taking steps backward at times, remember that it's all part of the intricate tapestry of self-discovery. So, if you find yourself in a moment of pause or retreat, know that it's not a setback; it's a pause in the symphony, a moment for reflection and integration. Embrace it as an essential part of your journey, for in these cycles, you'll find the seeds of transformation, waiting to bloom in their own time.

During these sleepy moments, it's essential to maintain some form of inner work, even if it feels less intense. Consistency, even in quieter phases, can have a profound positive effect on your jour-ney: it keeps you connected to the process and your inner self, ensuring that you continue to grow, learn, and evolve.

However, over time, as my awareness deepened and my understanding of these cycles grew, they became less turbulent.

With a newfound sense of compassion for myself, I began to navigate the ebbs and flows of inner work with greater ease. It was as though I had learned to dance in harmo-ny with these rhythms, embracing the highs and lows as integral parts of my journey. This grow-ing self-compassion allowed me to transition into a more consistent practice that extended through-out my days. Rather than waiting for the occasional "aha moment" to spark my inner work, I learned to infuse it into my daily life. It became a constant com-panion, a guiding presence that gen-tly nudged me toward self-discovery, even in the ordinary moments.

If you're already familiar with my work, you're likely aware of my steadfast belief in the transformative power of the 12 archetypes. These archetypes represent fundamental aspects of human existence, each endowed with unique traits, strengths, and challenges. In simpler terms, they act as the lenses through which we perceive and engage with the world.

Recognizing and identifying your primary archetypes marks the crucial first stride on the path of shadow work. You might won-der why this initial step is so significant. Consider this: Your arche-types serve as the hidden architects of your psyche, influencing everything from your responses to trauma, emotional reactions, and behavioral patterns. When you embark on shadow work armed with a profound understanding of your core archetypes, you unlock deep insights into why you react in specific ways, why certain wounds affect you more profoundly, and why recurrent patterns persist in your life. It's akin to possessing a map of your inner land-scape, granting you the ability to navigate this terrain with precision and purpose. This knowledge doesn't just ease the process of shadow work; it amplifies its effectiveness. Armed with a profound understanding of your arche-types, you can target the roots of your challenges and unearth the concealed aspects of your psyche.

The pivotal moment in my personal journey occurred when I stumbled upon the concept developed by Carl Jung. It was akin to discovering a treasure map to the profound depths of my being. I found that this awareness not only enabled me to uncover and heal long-buried traumas but also facilitated forgiveness towards individuals and situations that had once weighed heavily on my heart. It was as though I had encountered a guiding light within the labyrinthine depths of my psy-che. No longer did I feel adrift in the darkness, uncertain of my next steps, or leaping from one shadow work prompt to another. Instead, a newfound clarity and sense of purpose infused my in-ner work. I began to discern how these archetypes, these ancient and universal facets of human ex-istence, were not mere theoretical constructs but living, breathing forces within me. They served as the lenses through which I perceived the world and held the keys to unlocking my deepest wounds and greatest potentials. Concurrently, this knowledge provided a unique avenue to comprehend not only myself but also the motivations and behaviors of others. It emerged as a powerful tool for fos-tering empathy and compassion, enabling me to gain deeper insights into those around me and nur-turing more profound connections. This discovery was nothing short of an awakening—a pro-found realization that I was not alone in this journey but guided by some-thing greater than myself.

Gaining awareness of the hidden forces that shape our lives is an ongoing journey. It demands unwavering commitment and a profound willingness to be present, observing oneself with an open heart and mind. You listen to those inner voices, devoid of judgment, guided by compassionate curiosity. Daily dedication is the cornerstone of this transformative process. It entails observ-ing, recording, and reflecting upon your thoughts, emotions, dreams, and actions. Through this persis-tent exploration, you begin to uncover layers of your psyche that you may not have previously fathomed, yet they exert a profound influence on your life. This steadfast quest is not solely about identifying your archetypes; it's about forging an intimate connection with your authentic self and unlocking the doors to your true nature. Although the path may occasionally appear challenging, the rewards are immeasurable. By understanding and embracing the archetypes that guide you, you embark on the most direct route to healing past wounds, forgiving individuals and circumstances, and ultimately, living a life that aligns with your deepest values and desires.

Imagine the incredible transformation that could unfold if you dedicated a portion of your daily life to getting intimately acquainted with your authentic self. Picture this: each day, you take small, deliberate steps into the uncharted territory of your inner world. The power of consistency cannot be overstated. It's akin to tending a garden; nurturing it with a little attention every day yields a lush, thriving oasis over time. Similarly, in inner work, it's not the monumental leaps that wield the most transformative power, but the minuscule daily steps. The consistent practice of introspection, re-flection, and self-compassion turns the wheels of personal growth.

This is precisely why this journal has come to life—to serve as your companion on your journey of self-discovery. It's more than a collection of journaling pages; it's a guiding light. The pages of this journal are thoughtfully designed to lead you through the process of identifying your main arche-types and confronting the hidden aspects within. It's a tool that empowers you to recognize and in-tegrate the inner turmoil that might have been holding you back. Day by day, as you engage in your daily observations and reflections, you'll gradually unveil the path to self-awareness and emotional healing.

I've intentionally designed the journal and workbook as two distinct yet interconnected tools, offering you the flexibility to engage with them independently. While you can choose either one to start your journey, I strongly recommend using both for the most profound results.

One crucial point I'd like to emphasize is that, while this journal primarily serves as a practical tool, the accompanying workbook provides a deeper theoretical foundation and support: If you prefer a more hands-on, daily practice, this journal is an excellent entry point. However, if you're seeking a more comprehensive understanding of the 12 archetypes and are ready to delve into their intrica-cies, the workbook is a valuable resource.

The beauty of this approach is that it doesn't matter which one you begin with. The journal functions as your daily companion, guiding you through the ongoing exploration of your inner self. It provides a steady, consistent practice that helps you stay attuned to your emotions, thoughts, and behaviors in relation to your archetypes. On the other hand, the workbook serves as a valuable resource that allows you to dive deep into the intricacies of each of the 12 archetypes, providing comprehensive insights. It's essential to keep in mind that your psyche is a complex tapestry woven with multiple archetypal threads. Thus, as you engage in shadow work, you're not confined to ex-ploring just one archetype at a time. You have the freedom to choose your approach: you can delve deeply into the 12 archetypes, uncovering their layers, and then transition to the daily reflections to integrate them into your life. Alterna-tively, you can begin with the journal, gradually discovering the archetypes most present within you, and then dive deeply into the ones that resonate the most. Regardless of the path you select, what truly makes a difference in shadow work is your unwaver-ing commitment. It's your dedication to the process, your willingness to confront and embrace the hidden aspects of yourself, and your patience to navigate the cycles of growth that will propel you forward in your transformative journey.

As you embark on this journal-assisted expedition into the depths of your psyche, remember that every word you jot down, every thought you contemplate, and every emotion you explore is a building block in the construction of your true self. It's in the daily rituals of shadow work that you'll find the most profound revelations and healing.

As I conclude this introduction, I want to express that creating this journal has been a labor of love (and fun), born from a deep commitment to supporting you on your journey of self-discovery and growth. My intention is for these tools to impact your life in ways that you may not even imagine yet.

Your thoughts, feedback, and experiences are incredibly valuable to me. I invite you to reach out at **hello@booksquarepublish-ing.**com to share your insights and reflections. Your input can help shape future editions and resources, ensuring they continue to resonate with your needs. Additionally, if you've found value in this material, I kindly request that you consider leaving a review on Amazon. Honest and heartfelt reviews have the power to guide others on their quest for self-discovery, helping them find trusted resources in a sea of options.

I'm excited to announce that I'm starting a TikTok channel **@samanthahealingclub** where we can come together as a community. I invite you to follow the page, share your stories, and join in on the collective growth journey. Let's support each other, learn from one another, and continue expanding our understanding of the intricate landscape of the human psyche.

Thank you for choosing this journal as your companion.

Today ..../............./.............

Dear Self,

I embark on this journey of self-discovery with an open heart and a courageous spirit. I acknowledge the challenges that may arise on this path, and I promise to face them with unwavering determination.

I recognize that this journey may at times be difficult, as I confront aspects of myself that I have long ignored or hidden. But I vow to show myself the same compassion and understanding that I would offer to a cherished friend in times of need.

I understand that personal growth is not a linear path but a series of twists and turns, ups and downs. I commit to this journey wholeheartedly, knowing that it is through these challenges that I will grow and evolve.

I promise to celebrate every small victory, to be patient with myself when progress feels slow, and to honor the process as much as the destination.

With this journal as my guide, I am ready to delve into the depths of my psyche, to shine a light on my shadows, and to embrace the fullness of my authentic self. I trust that this journey will lead me to greater self-awareness, healing, and a profound connection with my true essence.

I carry with me the knowledge that, by embarking on this journey, I am taking a significant step towards living a life that aligns with my deepest values and desires.

With courage, compassion, and commitment, I am ready to begin.

[Your Name]

Exploring Your Main Archetype

This exercise is a crucial step in your inner work journey; it allows you to explore the profound impact of your main archetype and how it weaves through your life. Turn to the rear of the journal to pinpoint your core archetypes—the guiding energies molding your inner landscape!

Personal Stories

Share a personal story or experience that highlight the presence of your main archetype in your life.

Strengths

Write about the strengths and positive attributes that your main archetype has brought into your life. How have these strengths influenced your personal growth, relationships, or achievements?

Future Integration

Reflect on how you can integrate the strengths of your main archetype more consciously into your life.

Challenges

Explore the challenges or limitations that may arise from your main archetype's influence. How have these challenges manifested in your life, and what lessons have you learned from them?

Future Integration

Reflect on how you can navigate the challenges posed by your main archetype more effectively in your life.

How does your main archetype influence your daily choices and decisions?

Are there specific life situations or moments when your main archetype becomes especially prominent?

Have you noticed any changes in the expression of your main archetype over time?

Archetype Assessment Quiz

In this quiz, you'll have the opportunity to explore your own unique blend of archetypal energies. Think of these archetypes as timeless stories that live in the depths of your psyche, shaping your thoughts, emotions, and actions. By responding to a series of straightforward yes/no questions for each archetype, you'll gradually unveil the intricate tapestry of your personal archetypal energies. There's no predefined magic percentage of 'yes' responses required for identification; it's all about recognizing the patterns that truly resonate with you.

For a deeper exploration of each archetype and its role in your life, you'll find plenty of journaling prompts and guidance in the main workbook. These prompts will help you uncover the nuances and intricacies of each archetype within you, allowing for a richer understanding of your inner world.

THE CAREGIVER ARCHETYPE

Do you often feel a strong desire to take care of others?

Are you known for your empathy and ability to deeply understand others' emotions?

Do you find fulfillment in supporting and nurturing those around you?

Are you naturally protective of loved ones?

Do you often put others' needs before your own?

Are you drawn to professions or activities that involve caregiving or helping others?

Do you feel a sense of responsibility for the well-being of your family and friends?

Have you been described as a compassionate and selfless person?

Do you often offer a listening ear and emotional support to friends and family?

Are you comfortable in the role of a caregiver?

HOW MANY "YES"? ....

HOW MANY "NO"? ....

THE REBEL ARCHETYPE

Do you have a strong desire to challenge authority or question societal norms?

Are you drawn to causes that promote change and social justice?

Do you often find yourself pushing the boundaries of convention?

Have you engaged in acts of rebellion or activism in the past?

Are you known for your non-conformist attitude?

Do you resist rules or restrictions that you consider unjust?

Are you attracted to movements or ideas that advocate for individual freedom?

Have you ever felt like an outsider or misfit in certain social circles?

Do you express your unique identity through unconventional choices?

Are you driven to create change in the world around you?

HOW MANY "YES"? ....

HOW MANY "NO"? ....

THE HERO ARCHETYPE

Do you feel a strong sense of responsibility to protect others?

Are you often the first to step up in challenging situations?

Do you believe in doing what's right, even in the face of adversity?

Are you drawn to roles that involve leadership and taking charge?

Do you have a desire to make the world a better place?

Are you known for your courage and willingness to face danger?

Do you believe in the power of heroic acts to inspire others?

Have you ever been described as a natural leader?

Do you enjoy tackling difficult challenges head-on?

Are you driven to overcome obstacles and achieve great feats?

HOW MANY "YES"? ....

HOW MANY "NO"? ....

THE EXPLORER ARCHETYPE

Do you often seek new experiences and adventures?

Are you drawn to discovering the unknown, both externally and internally?

Do you thrive on exploration and embracing the journey?

Are you comfortable with change and unpredictability?

Do you have a strong desire to broaden your horizons?

Are you open to trying new things and taking risks?

Are you fascinated by different cultures and perspectives?

Do you enjoy traveling and exploring unfamiliar places?

Are you curious about the mysteries of the world?

Do you believe that life is a constant adventure?

HOW MANY "YES"? ....

HOW MANY "NO"? ....

THE LOVER ARCHETYPE

Are you passionate about building deep emotional connections?

Do you value beauty, sensuality, and intimate relationships?

Are you often guided by your heart and emotions?

Do you seek pleasure and enjoyment in life's experiences?

Are you drawn to romantic and affectionate gestures?

Are you comfortable expressing your feelings to others?

Do you prioritize love and relationships in your life?

Are you deeply affected by the emotions of others?

Do you believe that love is a powerful force in the world?

Are you known for your affectionate and loving nature?

HOW MANY "YES"? ....

HOW MANY "NO"? ....

THE SAGE ARCHETYPE

Are you naturally curious and eager to learn?

Do you enjoy analyzing situations and seeking knowledge?

Are you often the one people turn to for advice and guidance?

Do you value wisdom and intellectual growth?

Are you comfortable with introspection and self-reflection?

Do you believe that knowledge has the power to transform lives?

Are you drawn to books, documentaries, and educational content?

Do you enjoy engaging in philosophical discussions?

Are you known for your insights and analytical skills?

Are you a lifelong learner who seeks to expand your understanding of the world?

HOW MANY "YES"? ....

HOW MANY "NO"? ....

THE JESTER ARCHETYPE

Do you often use humor to lighten the mood in various situations?

Are you known for your playful and spontaneous nature?

Do you enjoy making people laugh and bringing joy to others?

Are you comfortable with humor as a way to cope with challenges?

Do you appreciate the value of lightheartedness in life?

Are you drawn to comedy and entertainment as a form of expression?

Do you believe that humor has the power to create connections?

Are you quick to find humor in everyday situations?

Are you known for your ability to improvise and be spontaneous?

Do you see life as an opportunity for fun and enjoyment?

HOW MANY "YES"? ....

HOW MANY "NO"? ....

THE CREATOR ARCHETYPE

Are you drawn to creative pursuits such as art, writing, or music?

Do you feel a strong desire to express yourself through creative outlets?

Are you often inspired to bring something new into the world?

Do you enjoy the process of creating and innovating?

Are you passionate about leaving a lasting legacy through your creations?

Do you believe in the power of art and creativity to inspire others?

Are you known for your artistic talents and imaginative thinking?

Do you find joy in bringing your ideas to life through creative projects?

Are you comfortable with the role of a creator and innovator?

Do you see creativity as a fundamental part of your identity?

HOW MANY "YES"? ....

HOW MANY "NO"? ....

THE EVERYMAN ARCHETYPE

Do you identify with the experiences and struggles of ordinary people?

Are you content with a simple, balanced life and relatable goals?

Do you value relatability, humility, and approachability in yourself and others?

Are you comfortable with your own strengths and limitations?

Do you appreciate the beauty of everyday moments and small pleasures?

Are you drawn to stories and characters that reflect ordinary life?

Do you find fulfillment in being relatable and down-to-earth?

Are you known for your ability to connect with people from all walks of life?

Do you see value in the ordinary and the familiar?

Are you at ease with the idea of being an "everyman" or "everywoman"?

HOW MANY "YES"? ....

HOW MANY "NO"? ....

THE RULER ARCHETYPE

Do you naturally take charge in leadership roles and seek to organize situations?

Are you drawn to positions of authority and responsibility?

Do you feel a strong desire to create order, structure, and stability in your life?

Are you comfortable making decisions that impact others?

Do you believe in the importance of establishing rules and guidelines?

Are you known for your ability to manage and oversee projects or teams?

Do you enjoy setting goals and objectives for yourself and others?

Are you drawn to leadership challenges and opportunities?

Do you see yourself as someone who thrives in roles of leadership?

Are you motivated to create a sense of order and control in your environment?

HOW MANY "YES"? ....

HOW MANY "NO"? ....

THE MAGICIAN ARCHETYPE

Are you drawn to the mysteries and secrets of the universe?

Do you have a strong belief in the power of transformation and change?

Are you comfortable with embracing the unknown and the mystical?

Do you often seek to manifest your desires and intentions through focused energy?

Are you known for your ability to see connections and patterns others may miss?

Do you believe in the concept of "as above, so below," representing the interconnectedness of all things?

Are you drawn to mystical and esoteric knowledge and practices?

Do you value personal growth, transformation, and self-improvement?

Do you see yourself as someone who can facilitate change and transformation in others?

Are you motivated by the idea of unlocking hidden potentials and mysteries?

HOW MANY "YES"? ....

HOW MANY "NO"? ....

THE INNOCENT ARCHETYPE

Do you often view the world with a sense of wonder and optimism?

Are you drawn to simplicity, purity, and a childlike innocence?

Do you believe in the innate goodness of people and the world?

Are you comfortable with a trusting and open-hearted approach to life?

Do you find joy in the beauty of nature and the small pleasures of existence?

Are you known for your ability to see the positive side of situations?

Do you value maintaining a sense of innocence and purity in your life?

Are you drawn to stories and experiences that evoke a sense of nostalgia?

Do you believe in the power of hope and optimism to bring about positive change?

Are you at ease with being seen as someone with a childlike innocence?

Traumas

This exercise forms a foundational step in gaining insights into your past experiences. Recognizing and distinguishing your past traumas is a vital aspect of the journey toward understanding and healing the wounds of your history. Pause for a moment to reflect on your life journey and the encounters you've faced. Contemplate those instances that have left emotional wounds or imprints. Once you've gathered some insights, it's time to categorize these experiences into two distinct groups: "Minor Traumas" and "Major Traumas." It's crucial to emphasize that this classification isn't based on the event's scale but rather on the emotional impact it had on you. Minor traumas may encompass incidents like disappointments, rejections, or conflicts. While less intense, these events still hold significance. Take time to reflect on how these experiences have influenced your thoughts, behaviors, or self-perception. Conversely, major traumas typically involve more profound emotional distress, such as abuse, significant loss, or life-altering crises. Dive deeper into exploring the long-term effects of these major traumas on your life, your relationships, and your overall well-being.

Small Traumas

Big Traumas

Shadow Integration

Self-Reflection and Awareness

Reflect on the shadow aspects you've uncovered through your self-discovery journey and acknowledge the emotions associated with each shadow aspect.

SHADOW ASPECT	EMOTIONS	THOUGHTS/BEHAVIORS

THE SHADOW WORK JOURNAL

Acceptance and Compassion

Cultivate a daily self-compassion practice that includes using affirmations, mindfulness exercises, and other techniques to nurture acceptance of your shadow aspects. For instance, take a few moments each day to offer yourself the same kindness and understanding you would extend to a close friend facing similar challenges.

Daily Affirmation

Healing and Transformation

Accountability, whether it's through self-discipline or with the support of others, can be a powerful force in helping you stay on track and avoid slipping back into negative patterns.

THERAPEUTIC SUPPORT	Consider seeking therapeutic or counseling support if necessary to address deep-seated shadow issues.	**Appointments Scheduled**
HOLISTIC PRACTICE	Incorporate holistic practices that resonate with you, such as meditation, mindfulness, yoga, or energy healing, to facilitate healing.	**D/W Practice Scheduled**
SUPPORT NETWORK	Connect with a support network or community that understands the shadow work journey.	**Community Involvement**
REVIEW AND ADJUST	Periodically review your shadow integration plan to assess progress and make necessary adjustments.	**Frequency of Plan Review**

Behavioral Changes

Outline specific behavioral changes or actions to integrate the positive aspects of your shadow into your life.

×··×··×··×··×··×··×··×··×··

Relationships

Examine how your shadow aspects have affected your relationships and set intentions for healthier interactions

×··×··×··×··×··×··×··×··×··

Milestones and Celebrations

Honoring even the tiniest of accomplishments plays an instrumental role in nurturing your personal growth!

MILESTONE	HOW I CELEBRATE	MILESTONE	HOW I CELEBRATE

Forgiveness

Forgiveness is a powerful act of self-compassion and liberation. By forgiving yourself and others related to your shadow aspects, you create space for healing, personal growth, and transformation. It's a process that can bring you closer to inner peace and acceptance, reducing the emotional charge connected to your shadows.

Forgivness Ritual or Exercise

Reflection and Growth

Take a moment to reflect on the remarkable journey you've undertaken, and the profound growth you've achieved by not only encountering but also wholeheartedly embracing this shadow aspect.

Inner Child Healing

This powerful journey begins with an Inner Child Visualization—a highly recommended practice prior to embarking on the forthcoming exercises. VThis visualization is instrumental in establishing a profound connection with your younger self, allowing you to grasp their emotions, needs, and aspirations more fully. Begin by finding a quiet, comfortable space where you won't be disturbed. Close your eyes and take a few deep breaths to center yourself. Now, imagine yourself in a safe and nurturing place from your childhood, a setting where you felt truly cared for and protected. Picture your younger self, perhaps at a specific age when you may have experienced pivotal moments or emotions. For example, for me, it would have been during my early adolescence when I grappled with the profound challenge of adjusting to a new school environment, all while seeking solace in the peaceful haven of my grandparents' countryside home. Engage with this visualization, letting it become vivid and real. Once you've connected with your inner child through this visualization, you're ready to explore the exercises in this section.

Core Wounds

x··x··x··x··x··x··x··x··x··x··

People Who Have Hurt Me

x··x··x··x··x··x··x··x··x··

People Who Were There for Me

x··x··x··x··x··x··x··x··x··

Inner Child Journaling

DIALOGUE

Dedicate a few minutes to write a journal entry from the perspective of your inner child. Let them express their feelings, desires, and needs.

ADULT RESPONSE

Respond to your inner child with the compassion and care of your present self. Offer comfort, validation, and support.

Day & Month

Meditation

Journaling

Self Care

Affirmation

Dream Analysis

X···X···X···X···X···X···X···X···X···X···X···X···X···X···X···X···X···X···

Setting:

Characters:

Events:

Emotions:

4 Things I am Greatful for:

♡ ♥ ::::♡ ♥ ::::♡ ♥ ::::♡ ♥ ::::♡ ♥ ::::♡ ♥ ::::♡ ♥

◉

◉

◉

◉

Charting Your Emotions Throughout the Day

	EMOTION	INTENSITY	CONTEST
Morning		⬤ ⬤ ⬤ ⬤ ⬤ ⬤ ⬤ ⬤ ⬤ ⬤	
Mid Day		⬤ ⬤ ⬤ ⬤ ⬤ ⬤ ⬤ ⬤ ⬤ ⬤	
Afternoon		⬤ ⬤ ⬤ ⬤ ⬤ ⬤ ⬤ ⬤ ⬤ ⬤	
Evening		⬤ ⬤ ⬤ ⬤ ⬤ ⬤ ⬤ ⬤ ⬤ ⬤	
Night		⬤ ⬤ ⬤ ⬤ ⬤ ⬤ ⬤ ⬤ ⬤ ⬤	

- ☑ Today, I feel _____ emotionally.
- ☑ This emotion was triggered by (specific event or situation) _____
- ☑ My initial reaction or response to this emotion was _____
- ☑ Accompanying this emotion were recurring or prominent thoughts about _____
- ☑ This emotion may indicate a hidden aspect of my psyche related to _____
- ☑ To address or understand this hidden aspect, I can take the positive action of _____

Daily Archetype Reflection

MORNING REFLECTION

Which of my main archetypes do I feel most connected to today?

_____

MID DAY CHECK IN

How did the archetype I identified in the morning show up in my interactions and decisions so far?"

_____

EVENING REFLECTION

Looking back on the day, how did the archetype influence my actions, reactions, and choices?

_____

Today's Wins
ooooooooooooooooooo

How I'll Improve Tomorrow
ooooooooooooooooooo

Day & Month

Meditation

Journaling

Self Care

Affirmation

Dream Analysis

×·–·×·–·×·–·×·–·×·–·×·–·×·–·×·–·×·–·×·–·×·–·×·–·×·–·×·–·×·–·

Setting:

Characters:

Events:

Emotions:

4 Things I am Greatful for:

♡ ♥ ⠿ ♡ ♥ ⠿ ♡ ♥ ⠿ ♡ ♥ ⠿ ♡ ♥ ⠿ ♡ ♥ ⠿ ♡ ♥

◉

◉

◉

◉

Charting Your Emotions Throughout the Day

///∽//∽//∽//∽//∽//∽//∽//∽//∽//∽//∽//∽

	EMOTION	INTENSITY	CONTEST
Morning		●●●●●●●●●	
Mid Day		●●●●●●●●●	
Afternoon		●●●●●●●●●	
Evening		●●●●●●●●●	
Night		●●●●●●●●●	

- [✓] Today, I feel _____ emotionally.
- [✓] This emotion was triggered by (specific event or situation) ....
- [✓] My initial reaction or response to this emotion was ....
- [✓] Accompanying this emotion were recurring or prominent thoughts about ....
- [✓] This emotion may indicate a hidden aspect of my psyche related to ....
- [✓] To address or understand this hidden aspect, I can take the positive action of ....

Daily Archetype Reflection

x···x···x···x···x···x···x···x···x···x···x···x···x···x···x···x···x···x···x···

MORNING REFLECTION

Which of my main archetypes do I feel most connected to today?

_____

MID DAY CHECK IN

How did the archetype I identified in the morning show up in my interactions and decisions so far?"

_____

EVENING REFLECTION

Looking back on the day, how did the archetype influence my actions, reactions, and choices?

_____

Today's Wins

ooooooooooooooooooo

How I'll Improve Tomorrow

ooooooooooooooooooo

Day & Month ....

Meditation

Journaling

Self Care

Affirmation

....

....

Dream Analysis

x··x··x··x··x··x··x··x··x··x··x··x··x··x··x··x··x··x··x··

Setting: ....

Characters: ....

Events: ....

Emotions: ....

4 Things I am Greatful for:

♡ ♥ ::::♡ ♥ ::::♡ ♥ ::::♡ ♥ ::::♡ ♥ ::::♡ ♥ ::::♡ ♥

◉ ....

◉ ....

◉ ....

◉ ....

Charting Your Emotions Throughout the Day

	EMOTION	INTENSITY	CONTEST
Morning		●●●●●●●●●	
Mid Day		●●●●●●●●●	
Afternoon		●●●●●●●●●	
Evening		●●●●●●●●●	
Night		●●●●●●●●●	

- ☑ Today, I feel _____ emotionally.
- ☑ This emotion was triggered by (specific event or situation) _____
- ☑ My initial reaction or response to this emotion was _____
- ☑ Accompanying this emotion were recurring or prominent thoughts about _____
- ☑ This emotion may indicate a hidden aspect of my psyche related to _____
- ☑ To address or understand this hidden aspect, I can take the positive action of _____

Daily Archetype Reflection

×···×···×···×···×···×···×···×···×···×···×···×···×···×···×···×···×···

MORNING REFLECTION

Which of my main archetypes do I feel most connected to today?

_____

MID DAY CHECK IN

How did the archetype I identified in the morning show up in my interactions and decisions so far?"

_____

EVENING REFLECTION

Looking back on the day, how did the archetype influence my actions, reactions, and choices?

_____

Today's Wins
○○○○○○○○○○○○○○○○○○

How I'll Improve Tomorrow
○○○○○○○○○○○○○○○○○○

Day & Month

Meditation   Journaling   Self Care

Affirmation

Dream Analysis

x····x····x····x····x····x····x····x····x····x····x····x····x····x····x····x····x····x····x····x···

Setting:

Characters:

Events:

Emotions:

4 Things I am Greatful for:

♡ ♥ ::::♡ ♥ ::::♡ ♥ ::::♡ ♥ ::::♡ ♥ ::::♡ ♥ ::::♡ ♥

◉

◉

◉

◉

Charting Your Emotions Throughout the Day

	EMOTION	INTENSITY	CONTEST
Morning		● ● ● ● ● ● ● ● ● ●	
Mid Day		● ● ● ● ● ● ● ● ● ●	
Afternoon		● ● ● ● ● ● ● ● ● ●	
Evening		● ● ● ● ● ● ● ● ● ●	
Night		● ● ● ● ● ● ● ● ● ●	

- ☑ Today, I feel _____ emotionally.
- ☑ This emotion was triggered by (specific event or situation) _____
- ☑ My initial reaction or response to this emotion was _____
- ☑ Accompanying this emotion were recurring or prominent thoughts about _____
- ☑ This emotion may indicate a hidden aspect of my psyche related to _____
- ☑ To address or understand this hidden aspect, I can take the positive action of _____

Daily Archetype Reflection

x··x··x··x··x··x··x··x··x··x··x··x··x··x··x··x··x··x··x·

MORNING REFLECTION

Which of my main archetypes do I feel most connected to today?

_____

MID DAY CHECK IN

How did the archetype I identified in the morning show up in my interactions and decisions so far?"

_____

EVENING REFLECTION

Looking back on the day, how did the archetype influence my actions, reactions, and choices?

_____

Today's Wins
o o o o o o o o o o o o o o o o o o

How I'll Improve Tomorrow
o o o o o o o o o o o o o o o o o o

Day & Month

Meditation

Journaling

Self Care

Affirmation

Dream Analysis

x·-·x·-·x·-·x·-·x·-·x·-·x·-·x·-·x·-·x·-·x·-·x·-·x·-·x·-

Setting:

Characters:

Events:

Emotions:

4 Things I am Greatful for:

♡ ♥ ::::♡ ♥ ::::♡ ♥ ::::♡ ♥ ::::♡ ♥ ::::♡ ♥ ::::♡ ♥

◉

◉

◉

◉

Charting Your Emotions Throughout the Day

	EMOTION	INTENSITY	CONTEST
Morning		⬤⬤⬤⬤⬤⬤⬤⬤⬤⬤	
Mid Day		⬤⬤⬤⬤⬤⬤⬤⬤⬤⬤	
Afternoon		⬤⬤⬤⬤⬤⬤⬤⬤⬤⬤	
Evening		⬤⬤⬤⬤⬤⬤⬤⬤⬤⬤	
Night		⬤⬤⬤⬤⬤⬤⬤⬤⬤⬤	

- ✓ Today, I feel _____ emotionally.
- ✓ This emotion was triggered by (specific event or situation) _____
- ✓ My initial reaction or response to this emotion was _____
- ✓ Accompanying this emotion were recurring or prominent thoughts about _____
- ✓ This emotion may indicate a hidden aspect of my psyche related to _____
- ✓ To address or understand this hidden aspect, I can take the positive action of _____

Daily Archetype Reflection

MORNING REFLECTION

Which of my main archetypes do I feel most connected to today?

_____

MID DAY CHECK IN

How did the archetype I identified in the morning show up in my interactions and decisions so far?"

_____

EVENING REFLECTION

Looking back on the day, how did the archetype influence my actions, reactions, and choices?

_____

Today's Wins

ooooooooooooooooooo

_____

How I'll Improve Tomorrow

ooooooooooooooooooo

_____

Meditation

Journaling

Self Care

Affirmation

Dream Analysis

x···x···x···x···x···x···x···x···x···x···x···x···x···x···x

Setting:

Characters:

Events:

Emotions:

4 Things I am Greatful for:

♡ ♥ ⸪⸪ ♡ ♥ ⸪⸪ ♡ ♥ ⸪⸪ ♡ ♥ ⸪⸪ ♡ ♥ ⸪⸪ ♡ ♥ ⸪⸪ ♡ ♥

⦿

⦿

⦿

⦿

Charting Your Emotions Throughout the Day

	EMOTION	INTENSITY	CONTEST
Morning		●●●●●●●●●●	
Mid Day		●●●●●●●●●●	
Afternoon		●●●●●●●●●●	
Evening		●●●●●●●●●●	
Night		●●●●●●●●●●	

✓ Today, I feel _____ emotionally.

✓ This emotion was triggered by (specific event or situation) _____

✓ My initial reaction or response to this emotion was _____

✓ Accompanying this emotion were recurring or prominent thoughts about _____

✓ This emotion may indicate a hidden aspect of my psyche related to _____

✓ To address or understand this hidden aspect, I can take the positive action of _____

Daily Archetype Reflection

x···x···x···x···x···x···x···x···x···x···x···x···x···x···x···x···

MORNING REFLECTION

Which of my main archetypes do I feel most connected to today?

_____

MID DAY CHECK IN

How did the archetype I identified in the morning show up in my interactions and decisions so far?"

_____

EVENING REFLECTION

Looking back on the day, how did the archetype influence my actions, reactions, and choices?

_____

Today's Wins

○○○○○○○○○○○○○○○○○○○

How I'll Improve Tomorrow

○○○○○○○○○○○○○○○○○○○

Day & Month

Meditation

Journaling

Self Care

Affirmation

Dream Analysis

×·⋯·×·⋯·×·⋯·×·⋯·×·⋯·×·⋯·×·⋯·×·⋯·×·⋯·×·⋯·×·

Setting:

Characters:

Events:

Emotions:

4 Things I am Greatful for:

♡ ♥ ⫶⫶⫶ ♡ ♥ ⫶⫶⫶ ♡ ♥ ⫶⫶⫶ ♡ ♥ ⫶⫶⫶ ♡ ♥ ⫶⫶⫶ ♡ ♥ ⫶⫶⫶ ♡ ♥

◉

◉

◉

◉

Charting Your Emotions Throughout the Day

|||❧||||❧||||❧||||❧||||❧||||❧||||❧||||

	EMOTION	INTENSITY	CONTEST
Morning		● ● ● ● ● ● ● ● ● ●	
Mid Day		● ● ● ● ● ● ● ● ● ●	
Afternoon		● ● ● ● ● ● ● ● ● ●	
Evening		● ● ● ● ● ● ● ● ● ●	
Night		● ● ● ● ● ● ● ● ● ●	

- ✓ Today, I feel .... emotionally.
- ✓ This emotion was triggered by (specific event or situation) ....
- ✓ My initial reaction or response to this emotion was ....
- ✓ Accompanying this emotion were recurring or prominent thoughts about ....
- ✓ This emotion may indicate a hidden aspect of my psyche related to ....
- ✓ To address or understand this hidden aspect, I can take the positive action of ....

Daily Archetype Reflection

x····x····x····x····x····x····x····x····x····x····x····x····x····x····x····x···

MORNING REFLECTION

Which of my main archetypes do I feel most connected to today?

_____

MID DAY CHECK IN

How did the archetype I identified in the morning show up in my interactions and decisions so far?"

_____

EVENING REFLECTION

Looking back on the day, how did the archetype influence my actions, reactions, and choices?

_____

Today's Wins

○○○○○○○○○○○○○○○○○○○

How I'll Improve Tomorrow

○○○○○○○○○○○○○○○○○○○

Weekly Reflections

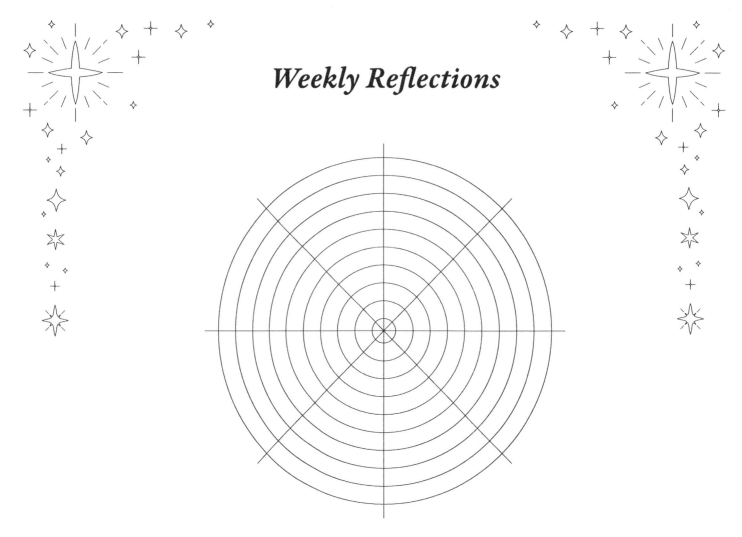

Emotions Wheel

×··×··×··×··×··×··×··×··×··×··×··×-

Assign one of your predominant emotions to each section and indicate the level of intensity for each emotion experienced during the week.

Emotion Spectrum

-									+

From Resisting Emotions (-) to Accepting Emotions (+). Mark where you fall on this spectrum for the week.

Comfort Level with Addressing Shadow Aspects

-									+

Fill in the "temperature" to represent your comfort level with addressing shadow aspects. A high temperature indicates greater comfort, while a low one suggests areas that need further exploration.

Shadow Dialogue

Initiate a weekly dialogue with one of your shadow aspects. Ask questions like, "What message did you send me this past week?" or "How can I better understand and integrate you?"

///~//~//~//~//~

Shadow Journaling

Write about the progress you've made, any challenges you've encountered, and your commitment to continuing this transformative work.

///~//~//~//~//~

Shadow Ingeration

Each week, choose a specific aspect of your shadow self to observe closely. Write about situations where this aspect may have influenced your behavior or decisions. Be honest and non-judgmental in your observations.

Aspects of Your Shadow

Reflect on how your shadow manifested through your feelings, behaviors, and experiences
in the events of the past week.

UNEXPRESSED DESIRES

DENIAL OF RESPONSIBILITY

MASKING AUTHENTIC SELF

PROJECTING UNWANTED TRAITS

Next Week Healing Plan

×··×··×··×··×··×··×··×··×··×··×··×··×··×··×··×··×··×··×··×·

SELF CARE

Plan a specific self-care ritual for the
week ahead. It could be a soothing
bath, a nature walk, meditation,
or any activity that nourishes your
well-being.

SET INTENTION

What emotional aspects or shadow
elements do you want to explore?
What self-care practices will you
prioritize? What emotional transformations do you aspire to achieve?

GOAL REVIEW

If you have personal growth goals,
revisit them. Assess your progress,
identify any obstacles, and adjust
your action plan as needed.

⬤ **Reviwed this week**　　　⬤ **Intention refreshed**　　　⬤ **Planned next week**

I want to take a moment to acknowledge the bravery and courage it takes to explore the depths of your own psyche and confront your shadow aspects. It can be a daunting and often uncomfortable process, but it is also one of the most rewarding and transformative journeys you can embark on.

Remember that you are not alone on this path, and that there is no right or wrong way to approach your shadow work. Be gentle with yourself, and trust in your own inner wisdom to guide you towards the insights and healing you seek.

I believe in your ability to face your shadows and emerge stronger and more whole than before. Keep going, and know that you are capable of great things.

With warmth and support,
Samantha

Fostering Healing Together

Our purpose is to support you in unveiling the depths of your inner world, to help you heal, to guide you toward self-awareness and your authentic self.

But our journey doesn't end here. It continues with you.

Your voice can light the way for others who seek the same transformation. If you have found any value in this material, please consider leaving an honest review on Amazon. Your words have the power to ignite change in others.

Let's not stop here.

We are building a vibrant community fueled by shared stories, mutual growth, and unwavering support. Join us on TikTok @samanthahealingclub to tap into a wellspring of guidance and exciting updates on upcoming projects and promotions.

We are honored to walk alongside you!

RECOMMENDED READING

In the realm of healing and personal growth, it is essential to have valuable reading resources that guide and inspire us along our journeys. I am excited to share with you a collection of books that have been fundamental in my own healing journey. Each book offers unique insights, practical tools, and transformative wisdom to support your transformation. I encourage you to explore these resources, I believe they can have a tremendous impact on your journey as well.

"Knowledge in a Nutshell: Carl Jung: The complete guide to the great psychoanalyst, including the unconscious, archetypes, and the self" by Gary Bobroff

Whether you are new to Jung's work or looking to deepen your understanding of archetypes, this book is an invaluable resource. Gary Bobroff presents Jung's theories in a digestible format, making them accessible and relatable to our everyday lives. What sets this book apart is its ability to bridge the gap between Jung's teachings and our personal healing journeys; beside presenting Jung's concepts, Bobroff also provides practical applications and exercises that allow us to gain a better understanding of the underlying patterns that shape our thoughts, behaviors, and experiences. By integrating and embodying these principles in our daily lives, we can experience profound personal growth and transformation.

"You Can Heal Your Life" by Louise Hay

Louise Hay's work has been an invaluable companion on my path of self-discovery, and it beautifully complements the process of shadow work by providing profound insights and practical tools for healing. I love its emphasis on self-love and positive affirmations. Louise Hay teaches us how to cultivate a nurturing relationship with ourselves and reprogram our subconscious mind with empowering thoughts and beliefs. By doing so, we open ourselves to immense healing and unlock the unlimited potential within us. This book serves as a powerful guide to embracing self-acceptance, practicing self-love, and creating a life filled with joy, abundance, and fulfillment.

"The Emotion Code: How to Release Your Trapped Emotions for Abundant Health, Love, and Happiness" by Dr. Bradley Nelson

Dr. Bradley Nelson's groundbreaking work in the field of energy healing has provided me with a fresh perspective on the relationship between emotions and our overall well-being. "The Emotion Code" offers a powerful method that perfectly aligns with shadow work by providing step-by-step instructions on how to identify trapped emotions and safely release them. By engaging with this book, you will gain invaluable tools to support your emotional healing and create a life of true alignment. Dr. Nelson's compassionate approach and practical techniques empower us to release emotional baggage, enhance our well-being, and experience profound transformation.

"The Gifts of Imperfection: Let Go of Who You Think You're Supposed to Be and Embrace Who You Are" by Brené Brown

"The Gifts of Imperfection" offers a powerful invitation to let go of societal expectations (which play a significant role in the context of shadow work!) and embrace our true selves with love, compassion, and authenticity. Brené Brown beautifully explores the impact of shame, fear, and perfectionism on our lives, while offering practical strategies to cultivate self-compassion and wholeheartedness. This highly accessible book creates a safe space for self-reflection and guides us to embrace vulnerability, celebrate imperfections, and cultivate a life of authenticity and joy.

"How to Do the Work" by Nicole LePera.

Nicole LePera, also known as The Holistic Psychologist, combines her expertise in psychology, neuroscience, and holistic healing to offer a holistic approach to self-healing and personal growth. In "How to Do the Work," she integrates engaging storytelling, relatable examples, and various modalities (including shadow work, inner child healing, emotional integration, and self-compassion) to guide us in understanding the impact of childhood

I HOPE THESE HELP!

experiences, attachment patterns, and societal conditioning on our present lives. This empowering book provides practical tools and exercises to support our healing journey, cultivate self-awareness, and create meaningful change.

 **"The Body Keeps the Score: Brain, Mind, and Body in the Healing of Trauma" by Bessel van der Kolk**

This book serves as a vital resource for those seeking to understand and heal from trauma. "The Body Keeps the Score" is a groundbreaking exploration of the complex relationship between trauma and our physical, mental, and emotional well-being. Bessel van der Kolk explains how trauma affects our brain, disrupts our nervous system, and manifests in physical symptoms and emotional distress. By understanding these dynamics, we gain the knowledge and tools to embark on a transformative healing journey. Van der Kolk's compassionate insights and practical approaches make this book essential for anyone seeking to heal from trauma and reclaim their lives.

 **"Awaken to Your True Self: Why You're Still Stuck and How to Break Through" by Andrew Daniel**

Andrew Daniel combines his expertise in personal development and spirituality to create a comprehensive roadmap for the exploration of the barriers that keep us stuck. "Awaken to Your True Self" provides practical tools to break through and embrace our true potential. Through insightful wisdom and actionable guidance, he challenges us to confront our fears, limiting beliefs, and self-imposed limitations, empowering us to step into our true selves and create the life we desire. This transformative book offers a path to personal growth, self-discovery, and liberation.

 **"The Mastery of Self: A Toltec Guide to Personal Freedom" by Don Miguel Ruiz Jr**

Through captivating storytelling and Toltec wisdom teachings, Ruiz Jr. illuminates the importance of self-awareness, self-acceptance, and personal responsibil-

ity. "The Mastery of Self" invites us to examine our belief systems, let go of outdated patterns, and embrace the power of conscious choice in creating the life we desire. Practical exercises, meditations, and reflections allow us to embody the teachings, empowering us to live in alignment with our true selves and experience personal freedom. Within the pages of this book, you will find a treasure trove of transformative wisdom.

WORKBOOK RACCOMANDATIONS

In my journey of self-exploration and personal growth, I have encountered a couple of self-love workbooks that have deeply resonated with me.

Self-love is not only essential but also foundational to personal transformation and growth. By practicing self-love, we establish a strong and stable foundation for our overall well-being, allowing us to experience profound healing and empowerment. Self-love empowers us to embrace our true authenticity, release self-judgment, and foster a deep sense of self-compassion. Through self-love, we begin to recognize our inherent worthiness and step into our personal power.

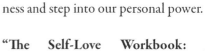 **"The Self-Love Workbook: A Life-Changing Guide to Boost Self-Esteem, Recognize Your Worth and Find Genuine Happiness" Dr. Shainna Ali**

 **"Self-Love Workbook for Women: Release Self-Doubt, Build Self-Compassion, and Embrace Who You Are" by Megan Logan**

What sets these particular workbooks apart is their comprehensive and compassionate approach to self-love. They address various aspects of our well-being and provide practical tools that support transformation. These workbooks have guided me in exploring the roots of my self-esteem, challenging self-limiting beliefs, and cultivating a positive self-image. Through engaging with these resources, I have discovered the significance of nurturing a loving relationship with myself, fostering self-acceptance, and embracing self-care as essential components of my personal growth journey.

Ready to Transform Your Journey?

WIN 3 ONE-ON-ONE SESSIONS

WITH ONE OF OUR TRANSFORMTIVE COACHES BY JOINING OUR TIKTOK CONTEST!

To participate, record a TikTok video where you share your workbook journey, highlighting your insights, learnings, and transformations. When posting, follow & tag our page **@samanthahealingclub** and DM your video link at **hello@booksquarepublishing.com**

Mark your calendars – the winner will be announced on our TikTok page on **November 2nd!**

Deepen Your Relationship

Open the door to boundless love by embracing the transformative power of shadow work as a couple

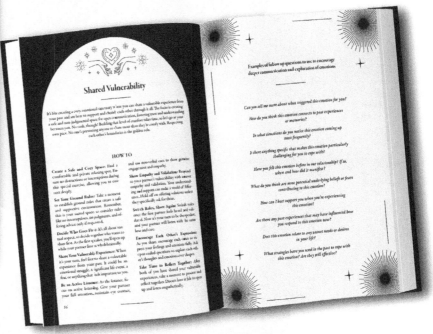

By journey together you will be able to forge a deeper understanding, empathy, and love that withstands the test of time

Made in the USA
Coppell, TX
12 October 2023